Everything You Need to Know About Soccer's All-American Girls!

Read all about them—America's women soccer stars. Learn why . . .

. . . Mia Hamm, Michelle Akers, Julie Foudy, and Carla Overbeck believe winning the 1991 World Cup gold medal was as sweet as winning the Olympic gold in 1996.

. . . Kristine Lilly calls their bronze-medal win in the 1995 World Cup "our wake-up call."

. . . Lorrie Fair suffered her greatest loss before the 1996 Olympic Games.

. . . Julie Foudy gave up a career in medicine to play professional soccer.

It's all here: a chapter for each player, including personal stats, her early years, life on the field, superstitions, pregame good-luck rituals, the significance of player jersey numbers, facts and favorites, and inspiration and advice to young athletes—plus sixteen pages of childhood, personal, and action color photos, answers to your questions, and much more!

Look for other sports biographies from
Archway Paperbacks

Derek Jeter: A Biography by Robert Craig

Michael Jordan: A Biography
by Bill Gutman

Skating for the Gold by Chip Lovitt

WNBA: Stars of Women's Basketball
by James Ponti

ALL-AMERICAN GIRLS

GIRLS

The U.S. Women's National Soccer Team

MARLA MILLER

AN ARCHWAY PAPERBACK
Published by POCKET BOOKS
New York   London   Toronto   Sydney   Tokyo   Singapore

AN ARCHWAY PAPERBACK *Original*

An Archway Paperback published by
POCKET BOOKS, a division of Simon & Schuster Inc.
1230 Avenue of the Americas, New York, NY 10020

Copyright © 1999 by Marla Miller

ISBN: 0-671-03599-1

First Archway Paperback printing June 1999

10 9 8 7 6 5 4 3 2 1

AN ARCHWAY PAPERBACK and colophon are registered trademarks of Simon & Schuster Inc.

Front cover photos by Zoran Milich, except lower right by John Van Woerden, center by Rob Tringali Jr./Sportschrome USA; back cover photo by Rob Tringali Jr./Sportschrome USA
Book design by Kris Tobiassen

Printed in the U.S.A.

QB/✗

IL 4+

All-American Girls is dedicated
to the past and present players of
the U.S. Women's National Soccer Team
who have cleared the path for the
next generation of WNT players.

★ ★ ★

Acknowledgments

A huge thanks to my daughters Jenna, Alivia, and Jessica Miller Mazura, whose passion for soccer inspired this book, and to their dad, Terry Mazura, whose knowledge of soccer and the "legals" associated with this project proved priceless. Thank you to coaches Tony DiCicco, Lauren Gregg, and Jay Hoffman and to the 1999 FIFA Women's World Cup staff, Aaron Heifetz and Brett Lashbrook. Thanks much to my agents, Annelise Robey and Stephanie Tade, for loving *All-American Girls* from the beginning. And to all the folks at Simon & Schuster, especially my editors, Liz Shiflett and Julie Komorn—it's been my pleasure.

Contents

Contents

★ ★ ★

Foreword

*A*ll-American Girls readers are in for a treat.
In the following pages you will learn so
much more about these extraordinary young
women who have made sports history twice—
the first time when they won the inaugural
1991 FIFA Women's World Cup, and then five
years later when they captured the gold medal
in the 1996 Olympic Games.

In 1991 I became the U.S. Women's National
Team goalkeeper coach. In 1994 I took on the
head coach position when Anson Dorrance
retired from international coaching. For a guy
who spent his life either playing with or
coaching boys and men, did I have a tough
time adjusting to women players? You bet I
did. If I ever wrote a book, the title would have
to be *The Mistakes I've Made*. From the beginning, though, guess who helped me bumble

through? My players did. Not only are they the best female soccer players in the world, these women excel in communication. What I learned, they taught me.

Not long ago I was asked to predict where women's soccer would be ten years from now. Easy answer. I want our country's girls' and women's soccer programs to remain in the forefront, serving as the model for the world. Not so easy to do. Our continued success depends on the development of youth soccer players. Our youth programs are good, but there's room for improvement. At the community level, coaches who emphasize "having fun" will foster a love for this game more quickly than if they emphasize winning. The young player who goes home after practice and kicks a soccer ball around in her or his backyard is a player who will improve simply because the game is fun to play. At the club level, I hope more emphasis will be placed on player development. Too often I see club players at the college level who still don't know the game. As far as the Olympic Development Program (ODP) goes, its primary function is to identify premiere players. Expanding its focus to give these players more playing time together will only strengthen ODP.

Foreword

The motto of the U.S. Women's National Team is Win Forever. In order to do that, we must continue to develop the caliber of soccer players found in the following pages of *All-American Girls*.

TONY DiCicco
Head Coach of the U.S.
Women's National Team

★ ★ ★

Foreword

When the writers of *Home Improvement* decided it was time for the Taylor sons to have a "passion" on the show, they didn't need imaginations to write my story line. Since age five, I've spent every available minute playing soccer. I started on AYSO (American Youth Soccer Organization) teams, then switched to club soccer when I was eight. Like a lot of serious young players, I dream of making the U.S. Men's National Team someday, but whether that happens or not, one thing I know for sure: I'll always be a part of this game.

My first contact with the U.S. Women's National Team happened when I met Mia Hamm. I was eleven at the time. She was filming a *Let's Play Soccer* instruction video. Since I was already known as the kid who loved playing soccer as much as I loved acting, I was asked to be in it. To be honest, I didn't know what to expect. The Women's National Team hadn't won the Olympic gold medal yet. I'd heard about them, but their games weren't televised, so I hadn't seen them play. The day I watched Mia Hamm film that video was the day I became a fan. As the 1996 Olympic Games approached, I looked forward to watching them on TV and was shocked when only a few minutes of their final game against China was aired!

For a long time my motto has been "think poz," which for me means work hard and set goals to be all I can be. The U.S. Women's National Team knows all about reaching goals through hard work. Their efforts have helped our country appreciate what many of us have known—millions of Americans love soccer. We come from everywhere. We are all colors and all races. Girls and boys play in equal numbers. Both deliver exciting games.

I'm proud to be a part of the book that profiles the players of the U.S. Women's National Team—members of the first generation of American soccer players whose amazing level of play has inspired the second generation to lace up cleats. We owe them a lot.

"Think poz"—

ZACHERY TY BRYAN
Actor, *Home Improvement*

★ ★ ★

Introduction

As it happened, the year the U.S. Women's National Soccer Team (WNT) made its debut (1985), my oldest daughter made her soccer debut. She was five, a brand-new AYSO (American Youth Soccer Organization) player. Founding WNT players were a bit older and included Michelle Akers, who is still going strong, recently scoring her one hundredth goal at a 1999 Women's World Cup qualifying match.

In the next few years my daughter transitioned from playing "swarm ball" to playing a game that looked a lot like soccer. Meanwhile, the WNT was going through its own changes. In 1986, while visiting an ODP (Olympic Development Program) regional camp, the WNT head coach, Anson Dorrance, spotted a group of players he took an instant liking to. He called them "the kids"—their names were Mia Hamm, Julie Foudy, Carla Overbeck, Kristine Lilly, Joy Fawcett, and Carin Gabarra. In 1987 he caused a ruckus by "cleaning house" to make room for them. Returning WNT players included Akers, the team's heart, and April Heinrichs, team captain, whose "take no prisoners" approach had formed the foundation of the Women's National Team. Dorrance and Heinrichs had met years earlier at the University of North Carolina at Chapel Hill when he coached her on the Tar Heels, the women's team nationally known for producing extraordinary soccer players. What Dorrance had noticed then about Heinrichs was her lack of interest in being liked. "April came in and absolutely tore everybody apart. Without remorse. She just wasn't willing to compromise her level of excellence to be mediocre but well liked," Anson Dorrance once commented. When she met "the kids," April Heinrichs met her kindred spirits.

For the next four years, the WNT trained hard, always looking for competitions and ways to improve. In 1991 they got the chance to show off their stuff at the inaugural Women's World Cup held in China. FIFA (the

Fédération Internationale de Football Association), soccer's international ruling body, had decided it was time to see what the women could do. The WNT made all the right moves and beat Norway, capturing the first Women's World Cup gold medal, an important victory for several reasons. First, in beating Norway, they beat a worthy opponent. Of all the competitors, Norway had the strongest record in women's soccer, supporting the sport since 1978. Second, the win earned "respect" from the American press. Michelle Akers said it best: "Before 1991 we couldn't buy press coverage. I'd wait around after games praying a reporter would show up. We knew without them we couldn't bring the game to the people. Winning the ninety-one Cup changed all that."

The World Cup win also attracted the attention of marketers. Finally, if soccer moms looked hard enough, we could find "WNT" imprinted paraphernalia to buy for our girls who had started talking about "Mia and Michelle" as if they were friends. The year 1991 also brought a change in the WNT's leadership when April Heinrichs hung up her cleats to coach, and Julie Foudy and Carla Overbeck took over as team captains.

Between the 1991 and 1995 Women's World Cup, the WNT continued gaining respect by winning important competitions. In 1994 Anson Dorrance retired from international coaching and handed the job over to Tony DiCicco, a U.S. Men's National Team goalie who had been the WNT's goalkeeping coach since 1991. Nineteen ninety-four was also the year the United States hosted the first U.S. Women's Cup, which the WNT won by beating Germany, China, and Norway.

By the 1995 Women's World Cup, my younger two daughters had joined their older sister on the soccer field and I began to notice changes. Club teams were sprouting up. Soccer clinics aggressively began to pursue girls for training sessions. In those few short years, my younger daughters enjoyed options my older daughter didn't.

In the following pages of *All-American Girls*, WNT players tell what happened at the 1995 Women's World Cup, and why they believe the devastating third-place showing was a weird kind of blessing, or "our wake-up call," as Kristine Lilly called it. Players will also share how they felt as 78,000 fans in Georgia cheered them on to the 1996 Olympic gold medal win.

As *All-American Girls* traces the WNT's path to the Olympic podium, it also traces the development of the youth soccer programs in this country. Like their faithful fans, the WNT players are products of these programs. Some players started on AYSO teams. Some switched to club teams as young as age eight. Some lived in communities that offered no girls teams at all. Some players were selected by ODP. Others were overlooked. Some had never heard of the program that has identified elite youth players since 1982, and some had to say "no, thank you" when that coveted invitation came, because their families couldn't afford ODP fees.

For one special week, this soccer mom tried her best to keep up as WNT players trained and competed in the 1998 Goodwill Games. In between training sessions, meals, team meetings, massages, shopping sprees— yes, these girls love to shop—and press conferences, I interviewed each member. Some told their personal story straight through, while others meandered down roads lined with memories.

Each story in *All-American Girls* is as unique as each player. A shared passion for this game has turned them into world champions and national treasures. Across the country, soccer moms and dads are grateful to the members of the U.S. Women's National Team. Their love for this team and each other makes them the best kind of role models for all-American girls and boys.

★ ★ ★

Michelle Akers

PERSONAL STATS

Position: Forward/Midfielder
Height: 5'10"
Weight: 150
Birthday: 2/1/66

SOCCER TEAMS

1970s–1980s Cougars Police Athletic League, Shorelake Thunderbirds, Union Bay Flyers

1984–1989 University of Central Florida

1990, 1992, 1994–present Tyreso Football Club, Sweden

1985–present U.S. WNT

*M*any mornings before players march into trainer Sue Hammond's hotel room to get ankles wrapped, Michelle Akers is there. Often, Michelle, the author of two books, sits quietly, computer on lap, writing, while Sue readies the supplies for the day. Sometimes they talk. Both have long histories with the WNT. Both have lots of stories to tell about the early years.

The one about their first tournament in France is a favorite. The U.S. Men's National Team, also playing in that tournament, traveled with them. A bus picked the two teams up at the airport and drove them to a bed-and-breakfast outside of Paris that turned out to be a damp old house with little hot water. Once there, the bus driver would not help carry the luggage. The women unloaded theirs, but the men disappeared. When the bus driver threatened to leave and not return the next day to take them to the stadium, the women unloaded the men's luggage, too. Says Michelle, "We needed that bus driver. This was a big tournament, and we weren't about to jeopardize our chances of playing in it."

So much for the glamorous athlete's life.

IN THE BEGINNING

Most everyone calls her Mish, but when the movie *The Lion King* premiered, Michelle Akers's thick mane of sun-bleached curls inspired teammates to call her Mufasa. The name stuck. When she was little, Michelle's sandy blond shock of curls almost always topped off a body streaked with mud. Her willingness to get dirty was why she played goalkeeper for her first soccer team. She was eight years old. Her mom was coach. They never won a game. Even then she hated losing. Says Michelle, "I cried after every game. I couldn't help it."

At the end of her first soccer season, the Akers family moved from California to Seattle, Washington. Michelle played on two teams there: first the Shorelake Thunderbirds and then the Union Bay Flyers. She credits both teams with teaching her how to play the game.

It was obvious by age twelve that Michelle Akers had all the right moves on the field. Off the field was another matter. Michelle experienced some troubled years that began about the time her parents divorced. She was in sixth grade. Her voice grows soft recalling the day she and her older brother, Mike, stood at his bedroom window and watched their dad move out. Says Michelle, "I was really rocked by it. We both were. I remember we slept in my mom's room that night."

After the divorce Michelle threw herself into soccer. Her efforts paid off. At age fourteen she was invited to join the Union Bay Flyers, an under-nineteen club team. She was also invited to join ODP, but her family couldn't afford it. The club team turned out to be her Olympic Development Program. Says Michelle, "I was playing up with great players who taught me everything I needed to know. I really didn't need ODP."

In high school she met a coach, Al Kovats, who became her mentor. He coached the boys soccer team at Shorecrest High School and let Michelle train with them. He also helped her find her faith. By then Michelle was playing stellar soccer, but her personal life was falling apart because of bad choices that led her down wrong roads, a journey she believes she had to take. She remembers the night Al Kovats drove her home after a practice. Says Michelle, "I sat in his car crying again about how I screwed up. We'd known each other for a long time by then, so I knew about his strong faith. That night I said to him, 'Ko, I want to become a Christian.' I walked in the house knowing that I'd be on punishment for the next eighty months, but somehow it was okay. I found something inside me that was stronger than anything else. Everything was gonna be cool. I just knew it."

For the next few years her soccer game only got better; Michelle married during this time. Then in 1991, after the WNT won the inaugural 1991 FIFA Women's World Cup, Michelle began to experience symptoms that left her feeling as if she had the flu twenty-four hours a day. For the next three years, as her symptoms got progressively worse, she searched for a diagnosis. During this time—a period she describes as "lower than the basement years"—Michelle also got divorced. Finally doctors diagnosed symptoms that included insomnia, inability to eat, severe memory loss, and crippling fatigue as Chronic Fatigue and Immune Dysfunction Syndrome (CFIDS). Little was known about the illness. To heighten awareness, Michelle appeared before a congressional committee on behalf of CFIDS victims. Says Michelle, "That was the first time I said out loud, 'I can't beat this.'" This was the first time Michelle Akers felt failure.

Although she describes her playing level

today as less than it once was, that level is still good enough. In the 1996 Olympic semifinal game, she scored the crucial tying goal on a penalty kick in the WNT's 2–1 victory over Norway. Her teammates call her the Grand Dame of soccer and speak in nearly reverential tones about her, the woman who was first among them to be confronted by negative voices insinuating women couldn't deliver an exciting game. Says Michelle, "I've never determined my life course by someone else's opinion. To those who said women couldn't deliver the goods, I simply said, 'Just watch me play.'"

ON THE FIELD

Michelle Akers plays forward and attacking midfielder. She compares her position to an American football quarterback. Says Michelle, "I either get the ball and score, or I pass it to a striker to score."

Until illness struck she led the WNT in goals scored. Her signature bombs to the net from impossible ranges have been clocked at over fifty miles per hour. Mia Hamm calls her the deadliest free kicker in the world. The press often uses phrases like "a hurricane pounding through" to describe her playing style. Comparisons to Mia Hamm are frequent. Michelle distinguishes their playing styles in this way: "I'm pure effort. Mia is pure grace."

The senior member of the team is a leader on the field. The role took time to develop. In the early years she wasn't vocal. Says Michelle, "I used to think my presence and work effort was enough, but I learned that in order to be a leader, you have to offer encouraging words." A smile curls the corners of her mouth. She winks. "And sometimes words that aren't so encouraging."

Best game moment: Winning the 1996 Olympics. Says Michelle, "I remember standing on the podium looking up to heaven. I could see all my family and friends from where I stood." She pauses. Tears brim her eyes. "It was a glorious moment I'll always remember."

Red card: She was red-carded once, in a game prior to the 1991 Women's World Cup. Michelle points to a grizzly-looking scar running down her left leg and says, "Before the Cup, everything that could go wrong went wrong. First, I fell on a sprinkler head and got this gash during practice. Then we played China and this player kept whacking the you-know-what out of me. I got the ball, she came up, slammed me from behind, and I fell on top of her." The Ref called the foul on Michelle, who said, "I got up screaming, so he red-carded me. Then Anson [WNT coach] ran out screaming and he red-carded him. The two of us watched the rest of that game from the stands."

Superstitions/lucky clothing/rituals: Michelle's only ritual is saying a prayer during the National Anthem before games.

In the zone: Says Michelle, "When I'm in the zone, just give me the ball. I'll do it. Just give me the ball."

Injuries: Opponents know when they come up against the 5'10" midfielder, there's no backing down. As much as her aggressiveness has defined her as a player, this same aggressiveness has also worked against her. Michelle blames "too much aggression" for at least some of the twelve knee surgeries, multiple stitches, and two missing front teeth she's suffered. Says Michelle, "I wanted to win so bad that I'd run over opponents even when I didn't have to."

WNT's first head coach, Anson Dorrance, used to say, "choose your moments," but it took getting sick with CFIDS for her to listen. Says Michelle, "Now, if I don't choose my moments, I can't stay in the game." These days if WNT is winning, Michelle isn't likely to do a diving header into a goal filled with opponents waiting to kick it off.

Jersey number: She's worn the number 10 since college. Historically, coaches reserve the number 10 for elite players like Pelé and Michelle Akers.

Blooper: "I do them daily," says Michelle. "I'm always putting my foot in my mouth by saying something I shouldn't say. I also trip over my feet all the time. There's too many to pick just one. It's constant, just ask my teammates."

SOCCER IS MY LIFE

At what age did Michelle Akers realize soccer was her life? She laughs and says, "Last year." Actually, soccer took top spot from the start, a fact that worried her father. Michelle played soccer as if there were a future in the game long before there was.

Says Michelle, "I remember Dad saying, 'After college, there's no place else to go, Michelle.' I knew he was trying to nudge me into expanding my athletic focus, but I couldn't. My blood and guts were in the game. I followed my heart. That's how I've always tried to live my life."

Then in 1985, when Michelle was a sophomore in college, her future opened up. The Women's National Team formed. She joined the roster immediately. When younger players Mia Hamm, Julie Foudy, Joy Biefeld (Fawcett), Carla Overbeck, and Kristine Lilly joined in 1987, they immediately looked to her for leadership. Until illness hit, she was the team's most recognized player. Getting sick forced her to change focus. She explains, "I had to come to terms with this very scary reality: if soccer was my whole life and I couldn't play anymore, what did I have left?" In the time it took to diagnose CFIDS, Michelle Akers redefined her priorities. Although still her passion, soccer now is a means to other ends. "Soccer gives me a platform for writing, sharing my faith, helping kids who need my help, and for educating the public about issues I feel passionately about, but it's no longer my only priority."

ON INSPIRATION

People who inspire are people with good hearts, according to Michelle Akers. Like her dad. When her parents divorced, he fought to stay in his children's lives. He never missed a game. He and stepmom Sue have followed her around the globe. Bob Akers also gave his daughter her best advice. She smiles. "Dad has always believed that having fun was the most important part of this game. Even now, he'll ask me, 'Did you have fun, Michelle?'" Today, his words are endearing to her. That wasn't always so. Michelle explains, "I remember this one game, I was probably nine or ten, we got creamed. I was so mad. I walked off the field, and there was Dad holding out my water bottle. 'Did you have fun, Michelle?' I wanted to yell back, 'That's a stupid question, Dad! Of course I didn't have fun. We just lost!' Instead, I just stormed off the field."

Michelle laughs when she describes her mom as "no June Cleaver." Her mother, Anne, is a woman whose own life showed Michelle that she didn't have to be locked into any one role. When Michelle was eight, her mom became the first woman firefighter in Seattle, Washington. Says Michelle, "She got tons of grief for it, but her dream was to be a fire-fighter, and nothing they dished out was gonna make her quit."

Offering inspiration to young people pleases Michelle Akers. In fact, she founded Soccer Outreach International for that very reason. The organization's goal is to use soccer to inspire the next generation to lead. Michelle says, "I'm always telling kids, don't worship sports figures just because they play their game well. Look at how they live their lives before you decide to follow in their footsteps."

ADVICE TO YOUNG ATHLETES

Her advice is simple. Says Michelle, "If you're true to your heart and listen to what your God is saying, you're going to be in the right place at the right time." After that, set goals. For those who don't have the ideal support systems, achieving goals is tough but not impossible. Michelle explains, "Parents of other players, coaches, relatives are all people who can help, but they have to know you need it." To parents, she offers this advice—make sure that the coaches who have so much influence over your children are people who have the whole person in mind, not just that part that wins them games. Lastly, Michelle echoes her dad's advice. "Soccer isn't brain surgery. Have fun. If you're not, figure out what's wrong and change it. This game should always be a joy to play."

FACTS

Caps: 126

Goals: 100

Assists: 36

Sponsor: Currently, none.

Causes: Founder, Soccer Outreach International (to find out more—home page is www.michelleakers.com).

Coaching/camps: Michelle Akers Soccer Camp, Tampa Florida, 1998; Northwest Soccer Camp, Michelle Akers Week, 1997 and 1998; Michelle Akers Week at Northwest Soccer Camp, Seattle, WA.

Awards (partial list): 4-time All-American, University of Central Florida; 1987 NCAA Final Four offensive MVP; 1991 FIFA World Cup Champion; 1991 FIFA Golden

Boot; 1995 FIFA World Cup Bronze
Medal; 1996 Olympic Gold Medal; author
of *Face to Face* and *Standing Fast*.

FAVORITES

Foods: Starbucks coffee, brownies, Mystic
Mints, B-B-Q, oatmeal.

Hobbies: Riding her Arabian horse, Vinnie;
reading; hiking.

Movies: *Mission Impossible, Babe, The Black
Stallion.*

Movie stars: Harrison Ford, Tom Cruise, Tom
Hanks, Rosie O'Donnell.

TV shows: Seinfeld, Animal Planet Channel.

★ ★ ★

Brandi Chastain

PERSONAL STATS

Position: Defender
Height: 5'5½"
Weight: 135
Birthday: 7/21/68

SOCCER TEAMS

1976–1984 Community and club teams
including Quakettes, Gators, Shamrocks,
Horizon, West Valley Soccer Club,
Crackerjacks

1986–1990 Cal. Bobcats, Cal. Tremors

1986–1988 University of California, Berkeley

1989–1991 Santa Clara University, Broncos

1991–present Sacramento Storm

1993–1994 Shiroki Serena (Japan League)

1991–1993 U.S. WNT

1995–present U.S. WNT

One afternoon during the 1998 Goodwill Games, Brandi Chastain took a van trip into Manhattan to promote the 1999 Women's World Cup at a press luncheon. With her were several WNT players, all in need of a little makeup. As usual, they depended on Brandi for supplies. As she passed out lipstick and mascara, Brandi's gaze fixed outside the van window searching for stores, specifically shoe stores. Telling teammates she was going shopping for shoes after the press luncheon made Kristine Lilly quip, "You can't possibly need another pair!" Of course, she needed another pair. Years ago Brandi's mom dubbed her "the Imelda Marcos of the U.S." because even then, Brandi's motto was, If a few pair are good, a few more are better!

IN THE BEGINNING

Not surprisingly, Brandi Chastain's first memories of youth soccer involved shoes. Her first pair of cleats were white with red soles and turned-up toes. Why turned-up toes? Brandi explains, "Back then, manufacturers made them like football player shoes because they thought we kicked with our toes, too."

Brandi, born and raised in the San Francisco Bay area, was eight years old when she joined her first recreational soccer team. Her team, the Quakettes, was named after a local pro team, the San Jose Earthquakes. Did the earth move when they stepped onto the field? Brandi can't recall, but she does remember picture day. "I had this Dorothy Hamill look going on, and Mom would fix my hair so cute. I remember our team banner behind us. That was always such a great day!"

Young Brandi had two sets of friends. With girlfriends she played house and other fantasy games; with younger brother Chad she played baseball with the boys. Says Brandi, "We'd have contests to see who could hit the ball over the house across the street." In sixth grade she joined a flag football team and played nose guard. In one game she sacked the quarterback. When she got up and looked over at her dad, Roger Chastain, he was beaming. As a former football player, he no doubt was thinking, like father like daughter. In high school Brandi's dad had played football while his future bride, Lark, chanted cheers to the crowd.

Some things never change. In the late 1970s Brandi's neighborhood team, the Horizons, transitioned to a club-level playing team. Her dad coached and her mom was the number one cheerleader. Not exactly soft-spoken, Brandi could never understand why her mom carried a megaphone to games. "She'd shout cheers through it and embarrass me like you wouldn't believe," recalls Brandi. Did she tell her to stop? Brandi smiles, "Sure, but it never did any good. You see, my mom is one of those soccer moms who considers cheerleading her sport. She knew the game, and when it'd get tense on the field, she'd get tense, too. She'd run up and down the sidelines revving up the crowd. Sometimes she'd get so wound up she'd kick at phantom balls!"

At age twelve, Brandi was noticed by the Olympic Development Program. She joined the ODP state team, moved up to the regional team, and at age sixteen was invited to an under-sixteen national team camp. In 1986 she enrolled in the University of California, Berkeley, where she played soccer with Joy Fawcett. The following spring she tore her ACL (a knee ligament). Says Brandi, "That's when the trouble began." Her injury, combined with a poor academic performance, eventually led to her dropping out of Berkeley, attending a junior college, then enrolling in Santa Clara University the next year. In between, in 1988, she joined the WNT, but in her first international appearance, she sustained another knee injury that kept her from continuing with the team.

The two seasons she played for Santa Clara were productive. Her team made the NCAA Final Four and she met her future husband, the university's soccer coach, Jerry Smith. In 1991 she rejoined WNT in time to play in the inaugural Women's World Cup. In 1993 bad news devastated her when then–WNT coach Anson Dorrance dropped her from the team. For the next two seasons she played in Japan.

After their third place showing in the 1995 Women's World Cup, WNT underwent major changes that began with a labor strike and ended a month before the team went into 1996 Olympic residency camp. During the strike, Tony DiCicco called her back to train for the 1996 Olympic Games, where Brandi Chastain played every minute of every game.

ON THE FIELD

When she first joined the WNT, Brandi played forward. When she returned in 1995, she was switched to defender. Transitioning to defense required her to develop patience. She explains, "As a forward, you run with a bit of abandon, so I had to learn to go easy. Defenders are a team's safety valves. When you play defense, your job is to settle things down, redistribute, or get the team out of tough situations. Midfield defenders create the calm before the 'flashes' up front storm through and score."

She's quite vocal on the field. Says Brandi, "I like to point out small, possibly unnoticed plays that create calmness or goal-scoring chances." Her ability to scope the entire field is why Brandi Chastain has been called one of the smartest tactical players in the game.

Best game moment: The 1996 Olympic semifinal game against Norway was a high point of her career not just because she played well—Brandi Chastain played hurt. She tore her MCL (a knee ligament) during the twelfth minute of the game. At halftime, she assumed the coaches would take her out. Assistant coach April Heinrichs asked how she felt. "I hurt bad," replied Brandi. "But can you play?" April wanted to know. Though she couldn't kick with the inside of her foot, Brandi believed she could still contribute. So did April Heinrichs, who told Brandi, "With one leg, you're better than what we have with two." Says Brandi, "Her vote of confidence inspired me to play my hardest."

Red card: Can't remember.

Superstitions/lucky clothing/rituals: Brandi never wears her uniform to the field. She likes putting on a clean jersey in the locker room right before game time.

In the zone: When Brandi Chastain is "on," she's having fun. Says Brandi, "I feel such freedom that I've been known to laugh as I dribble the ball down the field. I dominate and intimidate when I play in the zone."

Injuries: Torn ACLs in both knees and a torn MCL in her right knee all required surgery.

Jersey number: Number 6—no significance.

Blooper: The infamous divot story is one she can't live down even though it happened years ago during the 1991 World Cup. A newcomer to the team, Brandi was itching to play. During halftime she got the nod from the coaching staff. She was going in. "I was hyperventilating, that's how excited I was," says Brandi. At the midfield she received a through pass. With no one in front of her, she dribbled down the field. About thirty yards from goal, Brandi got ready to score. "I wanted to score so bad, the back of my heel could have touched my ear, that's how much of a back swing I had. Then I kicked it . . ." She stops speaking. And? "My kick was so powerful I took a divot of grass out that had to be a foot long." Instantly thirty thousand fans began to laugh. What happened to the ball? Brandi smiles. "I don't know where it went, but it didn't go in the goal." After the game WNT goalkeeper Amy Allman retrieved the divot and presented it to her as a keepsake.

SOCCER IS MY LIFE

When she planned her wedding in 1995, Brandi Chastain had no idea she would soon rejoin the WNT. She just knew she wanted to get married at Santa Clara University's historic mission church, and in order to do that, the popular chapel had to be booked one year in advance. Months after setting the date, WNT coach Tony DiCicco called her back to the team, so on Saturday, June 8, 1996, she married the head coach of Santa Clara University's women's soccer program, Jerry Smith, and the following Monday morning returned to residency training for the 1996 Olympic Games. Her honeymoon would have to wait. That's how much she loves the game.

She's been called "the comeback kid" in the press and for good reason. Her route and reroute to the WNT has been littered with hurdles high enough to derail most players permanently. Some of the hurdles were created by injury—Brandi Chastain has had three major knee injuries beginning with a torn ACL during her freshman season at Berkeley. Other hurdles were thrown up by poor judgment: when she began college, Brandi did not attack her academic challenges with the same energy she gave to soccer. Says Brandi, "I went from a small Catholic high school to this huge university. Some of my classes had eight hundred students in them. I figured the professor would never know if I was there, so I'd skip class figuring I'd catch up tomorrow. It didn't happen that way." In her sophomore year Brandi roomed with teammate Joy Fawcett. Unfortunately, Joy's work habits didn't rub off.

Recalling that time, Brandi says, "Joy was exactly as she is today. She didn't waste one minute. When she wasn't training, she was studying." The training part gave Brandi no trouble. In freshman year she earned *Soccer America*'s Freshman of the Year Award. It was the studying part that proved the challenge. Says Brandi, "There was so much freedom, I just wasn't prepared for it."

Knee injuries requiring surgeries added complications that eventually led to academic probation. Too far behind to catch up, Brandi Chastain left the university, moved back home, attended a junior college, and took a good look at her life.

The next few years proved to be a rebirth of sorts. Though she made the WNT in 1988, in her first international appearance another knee injury benched her. Healed from that, she began playing for Santa Clara University, where she met her future husband, Jerry Smith, the coach who taught her the importance of working hard. For a young woman used to having things come easy, the adjustment wasn't easy. "Jerry didn't give me a break. I never worked harder," recalls Brandi. The hard work paid off. In her years there Santa Clara made the NCAA Final Four twice.

Back on track, Brandi joined the WNT in 1991, but again she was derailed, first by another knee injury, then by WNT's coaching staff, who dropped her from the roster in 1993—a blow that was crushing but not fatal. Brandi took up the game in Japan and stayed in touch with the team. Then in the fall of 1995, fate interceded when the WNT, going through growing pains of its own, placed third in the 1995 Women's World Cup. Brandi called WNT's new coach, Tony DiCicco, and reminded him of her desire to return. He called back and asked if she'd consider playing defender instead of forward. Her reply was automatic—wherever the team needed her, that's where she'd play. In a speech made after the 1996 Olympic gold medal win, Coach Tony DiCicco called Brandi Chastain "a world-class defender and one of the best players in the world, period."

ON INSPIRATION

Growing up, soccer greats George Best and Pelé offered inspiration, and so did her family, especially her dad and granddad. Roger Chastain coached his daughter from age twelve to sixteen on a team called the

Horizons. Says Brandi, "That was his team. He gave us that name because to him, we were bright spots on the horizon." When the team began to travel to tournaments, several players had no way of getting to games, so Roger Chastain became the team chauffeur. Says Brandi, "He was willing to do whatever it took so we could get the best possible playing experience. He was a great coach." Her grandfather inspired her to be a team player simply by paying her more money for assists than goals. Brandi smiles. "He'd pay me a dollar for goals, but when I made an assist, he paid a dollar fifty!" Daily, WNT teammates inspire her. Says Brandi, "I feel younger every time I step out on the field with them. They are unique and special people. I love them."

ADVICE TO YOUNG ATHLETES

The best advice she ever received came from her grandfather, who lifted it from a Shirley Temple movie: "Be a tough little soldier." Says Brandi, "My grandfather would say, 'When you can't get something you want, don't give up, just work harder.'" Advice that came in handy, especially during those tough times she experienced on and off the field.

To young athletes serious about the game, Brandi Chastain advises them to spend lots of time alone with the ball. "Get familiar with how it rolls and bounces and feels. You can never do this enough," she says.

To all players, Brandi Chastain's advice echoes that of her teammates—have fun, it's a game!

FACTS

Caps: 79

Goals: 61

Assists: 16

Sponsor: Nike.

Causes: Humane Society supporter.

Coaching/camps: Santa Clara University camps and clinics; youth coaching, ODP

Awards (partial list): 1986 Soccer America Freshman of the Year; 1990 1st-Team NCAA All-American; 1991 Women's World Cup Gold Medal; 1991, scored five consecutive goals, her first international goals; 1996 Olympic Gold Medal; 1998 Goodwill Games Gold Medal.

FAVORITES

Foods: Thai and Mexican.

Hobbies: Shopping, movies, reading, golf.

Movies: *When Harry Met Sally, The Princess Bride.*

Movie stars: Billy Crystal, Meg Ryan, Olympia Dukakis.

TV shows: *Friends, 48 Hours,* sports programs, home improvement shows on the Learning Channel.

* * *

Lorrie Fair

PERSONAL STATS

Position: Defender
Height: 5'3"
Weight: 125
Birthday: 8/5/78

SOCCER TEAMS

1985–1988 AYSO Teams: Blue Streaks, Maroon Marauders, Killer Karrots, Killer Karrots II

1989–1996 RoadRunners, Sunnyvale Alliance Soccer Club

1993–1996 Los Altos High School Eagles

1994 U-16 National Team

1994–present U-20 National Team

1996–present University of North Carolina
   Tar Heels

1996–present U.S. WNT

The day after Lorrie Fair arrived in New York to play in the 1998 Goodwill Games was the anniversary date of her father's death. She took off one afternoon after practice with friends to find his boyhood home in Brooklyn, New York. "People told me not to go 'cause the neighborhood isn't so great, but I had to see it," says Lorrie. Standing in front of the two-story flat, Lorrie knocked on the door. A man answered. She introduced herself and explained why she was there. "He couldn't have been nicer to me. The house was definitely run-down but I was so glad to see it."

IN THE BEGINNING

The 1996 Olympic Games' alternate member of the Women's National Team was born a twin. Her sister Veronica is identical in every way but one: Lorrie is right-handed. "Ronnie's left-handed. I'm sure that's why she's so creative," says Lorrie, who is older by 32 minutes. Her sister also plays soccer at Stanford University for the Under-21 (U-21) National Team.

Growing up, the Fair twins' athletic abilities were constantly compared. Says Lorrie, "Ronnie is cool about it now because she's confident of her own abilities, but when we were little, sometimes it was hard on her." Lorrie describes her twin as a genius. She's no mental slouch, either. Lorrie attends the University of North Carolina and until recently majored in physics. The player, whom the Under-20 National Team coach Clive Charles calls a social butterfly, decided to switch majors when she realized spending time alone in a lab did not suit her personality.

Raised in Los Altos, California, with her twin sister and older brother, Greg, Lorrie also has a half sister and brother. Her dad guided her early athletic development. In fact, he wouldn't let her join a club team until it was obvious Lorrie favored soccer above all other sports.

At age fourteen, she joined Olympic Development Program's district team. By fifteen she was playing with the Under-16 National Team. At sixteen, she joined the Under-20 National Team and played at the 1995 Olympic Sports Festival, where WNT Coach Tony DiCicco was watching. He invited her to join a training camp held in August, after which he invited her to a September training camp and so on until it came time to choose the players for the 1996 Olympic Games' residency program. In December of 1995 she was selected to be an alternate, which meant missing her last semester of high school. Not a problem. She made up the courses and graduated on time just months before the 1996 Olympic Games. After the gold medal win she entered the University of North Carolina, where she plays for the Tar Heels during their season.

ON THE FIELD

In youth soccer, Lorrie Fair admits she was a ball hog. The behavior caused hard feelings among her teammates. Lorrie remembers a game when she stole the ball from her own player. She explains, "She was dribbling with her head down. I knew she had no sense of direction. I wanted to score, so I stole the ball away from her and scored!"

When she first joined the WNT, several players called her Little Squirt. Michelle Akers preferred the name Fairy. Though no longer a rookie, Lorrie still is intimidated by her teammates. She explains, "Before I joined this team, I was used to being one of the fastest and most skilled. Now I'm surrounded by these famous players, and it's kind of overwhelming sometimes." Her frequent feelings of trepidation were understood by WNT assistant coach April Heinrichs. Remembering the moment makes Lorrie smile. "April told me, 'Mia Hamm will not get mad at you if you steal the ball from her. The best way to earn their respect is to go out there and kick their butts!'"

As an attacking defender, she plays the left side of the field, where her primary job is defending. However, she is also involved in the forward attack.

Best game moment: She played club soccer for seven years. At age fifteen her team, the Roadrunners, won a National Championship. Says Lorrie, "It was such a big deal for us. We all grew up together. We were so proud."

Red card: Lorrie received two yellow cards in one high school game, the equivalent to one red card.

Superstitions/lucky clothing/rituals: Before games, Lorrie puts on left-sided garments first—left sock, left shinguard, etc. Why? "I don't know," she replies.

In the zone: "It's total confidence. My focus is intense, but I'm not stressed at all. I feel free," Lorrie says.

Injuries: a torn MCL (a knee ligament), a common soccer player injury.

Jersey number: Jersey number 2 has no significance.

Blooper: Minutes before a club team game, the referee did a player numbers check. She had to pull down her sweatpants for him to see her number and that was when she remembered. Lorrie smiles. "I felt this cold breeze and then heard parents laughing. I forgot to put on my soccer shorts and I was wearing Daffy Duck underwear!"

ON INSPIRATION

Her father died of a heart attack right before Lorrie was selected for the ODP district team. Growing up, his support always inspired her to excel. She smiles, "Even when I was hogging the ball and getting in trouble with my teammates, Dad couldn't help but smile. He'd say, 'Lorrie, stay in position,' but I knew, down deep, he was so proud of me and the way I played."

ADVICE TO YOUNG ATHLETES

She passes along the worst advice she ever received and warns: don't believe everything you hear. During her second AYSO season, a coach told her not to be so aggressive. She recalls the moment and says, "You know, that has stuck with me. When I was real little, I used to be fearless. I don't think I've ever gotten that level of aggression back. His words hurt me as a player."

★   ★   ★

FACTS

Caps: 35

Goals: 1

Assists: 1

Sponsor: College students cannot have sponsors, according to NCAA rules.

Coaching/camps: Against NSCAA rules for college players to coach.

Awards: 1996–97 member of NCC academic honor roll; 2-time Parade All-American;

2-time NSCAA All-American; 1996
Olympic Gold Medal; 1998 Goodwill
Games Gold Medal.

FAVORITES

Foods: Pizza.

Hobbies: People watching, stargazing.

Movies: *The Usual Suspects, Armageddon.*

Movie stars: Val Kilmer, Robin Williams, Meg
Ryan.

TV shows: *South Park, Friends, Ally McBeal,
Seinfeld.*

$\star$ $\star$ $\star$

Joy Fawcett

PERSONAL STATS

Position: Defender/Midfielder
Height: 5'5"
Weight: 130
Birthday: 2/8/68

SOCCER TEAMS

1975–1976 Green Mean Machine
1982–1986 Hotspurs Club Team
1986–1989 University of California, Berkeley
1987–1989 Tremor Soccer Club
1987–present U.S. WNT

When Joy Fawcett hits the road with the WNT, her two daughters go, too. They have their routine down pat. Each morning after breakfast, a bus takes Mom to practice. Preschooler Katelyn and toddler Carli stay at the hotel with a sitter, usually Grandma Biefeld, Joy's mom. When practice ends, the bus delivers her back to the hotel, where the girls are always waiting. Katelyn, the oldest, will run up to Mom unless one of her adopted "aunts" happens to step off the bus first. Carli sits in her umbrella stroller waiting. The instant she spots Joy, Carli wants "up" and Katey gets busy planning their afternoon. Maybe they'll swim in the hotel pool or maybe they'll take a van ride to the mall. What's certain is Joy won't have time alone, at least not until the Sandman makes his nightly visit. Too often, he arrives late. There's only one glitch in Joy Fawcett's home-on-the-road routine: bedtime. That's when she misses her husband, Walt, most. At home Daddy takes care of tucking the kids in.

Joy shrugs hopelessly. "I don't know how he does it, but he always gets them to sleep right away. I never can."

IN THE BEGINNING

Joy Fawcett is usually photographed with her thick brown hair pulled back tight into a ponytail perched high on her head. She calls herself shy. During childhood, whenever she tried something new, a bad case of nerves would hit. Playing soccer always set them off, and they fluttered inside her stomach like butterflies. One day before a game Joy tried to describe the feeling to her older sister. "I got fleas," she said. From that day on, her family and teammates called her Flea. Finally, in high school, they stopped.

Joy grew up in Huntington Beach, California, where kids either played soccer, surfed, or both. Joy is the fourth oldest of Beverly and Terry Biefeld's brood of nine children. Except for her foster brother, all played soccer. Four earned soccer scholarships to college. Older brother Eric also played for the U.S. Men's National Team.

Like her teammates, Joy's athletic talents sprouted early. She was fast, so naturally, youth soccer coaches played her at forward. Joy played at the community level until her team turned into a club team. She stayed with them through high school even though they weren't very good. Explains Joy, "I was asked to join other teams, but winning wasn't my priority. My teammates were my friends. We had so much fun playing together."

Joy was twelve or thirteen when she made the Under-14 Olympic Development Program's district team. She almost missed the opportunity. Joy says, "I didn't know anyone, so I didn't want to go. My coach dragged me there."

Joy loved the experience because it challenged her to become better. "That's where I learned how to juggle. They had us juggling forever. I got pretty good at it," Joy says. Good enough to make the ODP state team where she met Julie Foudy, another Orange County, California, girl who showed great promise. At first Joy was intimidated by Julie. Why? She explains, "I didn't believe I matched up."

But she did. Both girls made ODP's Regional Team, which in the early 1980s only existed on paper. The team never played together. Though she had risen to the top of the state ODP roster, Joy had no dream of joining the national team for one simple reason: it didn't exist. Joy says, "Back then I just hoped soccer would help me get a good education. That was my only dream."

The WNT formed in 1985. When Joy made the Junior National Team in 1986, she started dreaming. Her new teammates included Julie Foudy, Mia Hamm, Carla Overbeck, and Kristine Lilly. A stroke of good luck made the dream more real. The WNT played in a tournament that needed a fourth team. With no other national teams available, the U.S. Junior National Team was invited. They ended up faring better than their senior counterparts. What happened next surprised Joy. "Anson [then WNT coach] asked us to join the team. It was a shock. I didn't see it coming."

The year was 1987. The U.S. Women's National Team was two years old.

ON THE FIELD

Older WNT players still call her Beef (short for Biefeld), Julie Foudy calls her Joyful, younger players call her Joy, and coach Tony DiCicco surprised Joy by calling her "the best defender in the world." She says, "My team has many fine defenders so when Tony said that, I was honored. I've never wanted to be just a good player. I've always wanted to be the best."

She didn't start out playing defense. Through high school she played forward. In college her coaches moved her to the midfield, a transition that wasn't too jarring because she still played offense. When she joined the WNT, coaches moved her to defender. That switch took time adjusting to. Why? Joy explains, "I love being involved in the attack. That's what I missed the most. I still do."

Joy plays right side defender. Responsibilities include denying opponents possession of the ball when they enter her zone, providing cover for teammates, and starting the attack forward.

The press often describes her as a finesse player. Joy defines her style as clean. "I'm not very physical. Even as a child I wasn't." When she first joined the WNT, coaches initially considered her lack of physical contact a negative, but Joy's talent changed minds. Coach Tony DiCicco describes her this way: "She doesn't rock you with hard crushing tackles . . . she's more graceful than that. She just picks your pocket as she goes by."

For five years Joy coached UCLA's women's soccer team. The daily round-trip took four hours. She decided to quit when the job began to interfere with her ability to train properly. Says Joy, "There are too many good players coming up wanting your spot. Playing at this level has to be a full-time job." After all these years, does Joy Fawcett still question her place on the team? Joy answers emphatically, "At this level you learn quick—nothing is a given."

Someday she hopes to coach in the professional women's soccer league, that is, after she plays in it. Her opinion about the formation of a league echoes that of teammates, especially the senior members who hear their playing clocks tick down. Says Joy, "Everything is in place. Now we need the league. I just hope it happens in time for me to play."

Best game moment: In the final game against China in the 1996 Olympics, Joy Fawcett passed the ball to Tiffeny Milbrett, who shot the goal and won the game. For sure, that was her finest moment. Joy says, "When I look at the tape, it was a much longer run than I remember. I didn't think I had the right angle to shoot from, but I wasn't sure. I remember thinking 'Shoot or pass? Shoot or pass?' I didn't see Millie but I heard her. I passed it and she shot it in. It was glorious!"

Did passing the ball without seeing Tiffeny Milbrett add to the tension? Joy answers no. "The beauty of this team is that we are there for each other. If I'm busting my butt to get down the field, I know my teammates are busting butt to be there. That comes with years of playing together. I heard Millie's voice, that was enough. I knew she was there."

Red card: None.

Superstitions/lucky clothing/rituals: Her only ritual, besides drinking a can of Diet Coke and eating a peanut butter and jelly sandwich before game time, is wearing comfortable underwear. She blushes. "I always make sure my underwear fits just right. I hate the kind that give you a wedgie!"

In the zone: Intense games trigger the shift. Says Joy, "I become very different. I'm talking, I'm giving directions, offering support. I'm totally there."

Injuries: None. Joy says, "The only thing I've ever worked back from were my two pregnancies."

Jersey number: The number 5 has always been the Biefeld family's soccer jersey number. Everyone wore it. When Joy joined WNT, 5 was taken, so she chose 14. When 5 became available again, she didn't want it. Joy explains, "I had too much good luck with 14 by then."

Blooper: No one blooper stands out. Missed headers and tripping over her feet on the field happen too often to remember just one.

SOCCER IS MY LIFE

Joy ran track in high school mainly to stay fit. Her first passion was always soccer, a passion tested in high school. Joy's speed made her a star player on the track team. During senior year the team made it to the playoffs, but the meet conflicted with an ODP game. When she told her track coach she couldn't go, he threatened to kick her off the team. Her reply was automatic: ODP came first. He carried the threat further. If she didn't show up, he would make sure she didn't graduate Athlete of the Year. Her answer still didn't change. Though everyone expected her to, Joy Biefeld did not graduate Athlete of the Year from her high school.

Her unwavering commitment to the game didn't erase the fact that Joy hated spending nights away from family. A few times her need to be home interfered with soccer opportunities. At fourteen she was invited to attend an ODP Under-16 camp in San Diego. She was thrilled and petrified. She had never spent a week away from home. Joy laughs, her head shaking slowly, "I didn't make it. Dad had to come get me."

When time came to apply to colleges, her parents hoped she'd stick close to home, but Joy wanted to play soccer at the University of North Carolina. She wrote Coach Anson Dorrance a letter expressing that desire. His response? Joy laughs again. "He never wrote back. To this day, I razz him about that."

She attended the University of California, Berkeley, a day's drive away. Homesickness followed her. Says Joy, "My first year was a nightmare. I cried every day." Life looked better by sophomore year. Joy became a starter on Berkeley's soccer team, and she joined the WNT. During college, her team made it to the NCAA Final Four twice.

Determination to do well in school and soccer kept Joy focused. She graduated with a degree in physical education. Of those years Joy says, "I studied, practiced, and played, period." Until she met her future husband, Walter Fawcett. They met at the end of sophomore year, but he had a girlfriend at the time. In junior year she got a phone call. It was Walter. Now unattached, he asked if she would like to go out. Joy said yes, then told him what he'd get used to hearing: she was leaving for training camp the next day, and after camp she was off to Europe for several weeks. Their date would have to wait. Walter Fawcett wasn't willing. One day, unannounced, he showed up at her camp. That night they had their first date. One year after graduation they married— on June 15, 1991.

After five years of coaching at UCLA, Joy quit and took on an Under-14 club team closer to home. Now that daughter Katey is beginning to play, Joy says she'd like to coach her, too. At the pee-wee level? Joy laughs, "Sure, why not?"

She may have her chance soon. It looks as if Katey is getting the soccer bug. Up until recently the preschooler insisted she was going to be a "cooker" at McDonald's when she grew up, but when she discovered soccer, a conflict arose in her mind. Joy explains, "She came in the kitchen one day after playing and said, 'Mom, do you think I can be a cooker at McDonald's at night and play soccer during the day?'"

What was Mom's answer? Joy grins. "I said I thought she could do both."

Like mother, like daughter.

ON INSPIRATION

Joy Biefeld Fawcett's siblings' exceptional soccer-playing abilities always gave her the inspiration to work harder growing up. Her parents also inspire her. Joy says, "They are wonderful people. I strive to be like them." Her mother's help with the children earns her highest praise. "I couldn't do any of this without her."

When Joy gave birth to her first child in 1994 and returned to the lineup, she instantly became an inspiration for women athletes. This fact delights her. Unlike other WNT teammates who retired to have children, Joy wanted to start her family—she hopes for five—but she wasn't ready to retire. Doubts plagued her throughout the pregnancy. Says Joy, "It was scary, especially when I'd watch the team play. I'd think, they don't need me anymore."

With her doctor's guidance, she developed a training regime. Teammates supported her throughout the nine months—except one time. Joy laughs. "I trained with them until I started showing, then I stopped. But this one day I really felt like scrimmaging. In unison they all yelled, 'No way!'"

ADVICE TO YOUNG ATHLETES

Joy likes to pass on to children the best advice she ever received: do your best. No one can ask for more. To parents, her advice centers on coaches. Joy cautions, "Beware of overzealous coaches. They can break a spirit and burn a player out. I've seen it happen, and once you kill a child's love for the game, it's over."

FACTS

Caps: 126

Goals: 17

Assists: 13

Sponsor: Adidas.

Causes: Smoke-Free Kids, a soccer anti-smoking campaign.

Coaching/camps: Julie Foudy Soccer Camp coach.

Awards (partial list): 1991 FIFA World Cup winner; 1995 FIFA World Cup Bronze Medal; 1996 Olympic Gold Medal; 1997 Pacific 10 Coach of the Year Award; 1998 Goodwill Games Gold Medal.

FAVORITES

Food: Spaghetti, cinnamon sugar pretzels, barbecue ribs.

Hobbies: Reading, Rollerblading, shopping, cross-stitching.

Movie star: Mel Gibson.

Movies: *Pretty Woman, Lethal Weapon, Ever After.*

TV shows: *Seventh Heaven, Frazier, ER.*

★ ★ ★
Julie Foudy

PERSONAL STATS

Position: Central midfielder
Height: 5'6"
Weight: 130
Birthday: 1/23/71

SOCCER TEAMS

1978–1979 The Strikers
1979–1988 The Mission Viejo Soccerettes
1989–1990 The Nitemares
1989–1993 Stanford University Cardinals
1987–present U.S. WNT

*B*efore hitting the field for a Goodwill Games *practice, WNT players received brand-new soccer socks. Julie Foudy pulled on a pair, discovered them a tad too long, and became inspired. Hiking the usual knee-high socks up to their mid-thigh length, she pulled her shorts down to "gangsta" length, hollered, "Hike 'em up, girls, and follow me!" and sauntered out to the field. The scary part? Several players followed her.*

IN THE BEGINNING

"Lil calls me Loudy Foudy 'cause I'm not exactly the quiet type," Julie Foudy says. That nickname is one of several teammates call the co-captain of the WNT. Fruity Foudy, Jules, Foud, and Rowdy Foudy are a few more.

With curly brown hair, baby-blue-eyed Julie Foudy is a born practical joker who possesses not one shy bone. The WNT player most often before the cameras, Julie is quite comfortable speaking to anyone. She loves to sing and will belt out songs on the bus, at dinner, or walking down a hotel corridor. Rarely does she finish a number—that would require knowing the lyrics, and usually Julie only knows the first few lines.

Her passion for doughnuts is well documented. Days after the 1996 Olympic win, she fessed up on *Late Night with Conan O'Brien* that Krispy Kreme's warm-glazed doughnuts and Dunkin' Donuts' chocolate glazed doughnut holes were favorites. The obsession began early. Somehow, eating doughnuts paired perfectly with soccer and church in young Julie Foudy's mind. The church connection was obvious. Not a sit-still-for-an-hour kind of kid, the promise of doughnuts must have been the prize. But wolfing down doughnuts before games? Surely, she required no energy boost. By her own admission, Julie was a hyper child who found sports the ideal outlet for her limitless energy.

Julie grew up with two older brothers and one sister in Orange County, California. They all played sports—football, volleyball, basketball, and softball—but none played much soccer. She smiles, "Except to hear them talk, they'd have you believing they taught me everything I know."

Her first soccer teammates were boys. She was six and a first grader when a group invited her to play at recess. It was instant love. Because her community's soccer entry level was seven, Julie had to wait. When she finally joined a team, she bought white cleats and wore them until the cleats wouldn't grip anymore.

At age eight Julie joined a club team, the Soccerettes. She stayed with them for ten years and won several titles including a national title. Her club coach told Julie about the Olympic Development Program. Says Julie, "I had no idea what it was. He told us about tryouts. Four of us went, for the fun of it, really. We all made the district team."

She made the ODP U-19 regional team in her high school sophomore year. In the summer of 1987 the four ODP regional teams joined up at a National Team training camp in Michigan. There she met Mia Hamm, Carla Overbeck, Joy Fawcett, Kristine Lilly, and Linda Hamilton (retired WNT player). At the end of the two weeks, then–WNT coach Anson Dorrance invited "the kids"— his name for them—to join the Junior National Team, which was scheduled to play in a tournament immediately following the camp. The Women's National Team also competed in that tournament, but the juniors fared better. Coach Anson Dorrance noticed. He asked "the kids" to join the WNT for a tournament in China. Julie says, "In a matter of one summer, I went from playing on an ODP team to the Women's National Team." She was sixteen years old and entering her junior year of high school.

For the next two years she juggled the demands of the WNT with the demands of high school, which included playing varsity soccer. The tough schedule taught her how to structure time. Says Julie, "I always got better grades during soccer season because I knew I couldn't procrastinate."

When time came to choose a college, Julie was offered several scholarships, including one to the University of North Carolina at Chapel Hill, home of WNT coach Anson Dorrance's Tar Heels, the best women's soccer team in the country. Turning down UNC was not easy. The Tar Heels' top players included Mia Hamm and Kristine Lilly.

But Julie had a dream. Since childhood, she had wanted to attend Stanford University on a soccer scholarship. Problem was, Stanford didn't offer soccer scholarships at that time. If she went there, the Foudys would have to pay the private school tuition. Was it fair to ask her parents to pay tuition when good schools were offering scholarships?

Julie's parents urged her to ignore the

money factor. Julie laughs, "They even said, 'We'll sell the house and kids if we have to!'" Still, ignoring money when it wasn't falling off the Foudy family tree was not easy for this very responsible high school senior to do.

Then came a sign. At the time Julie needed to notify colleges, the Foudys moved. Up in her room packing one afternoon, she came across Bertha, her diary from fourth grade. On page 1, written seven years earlier, was this entry:

Mrs. Miller wanted me to make a New Year's resolution list, so here it is.
1. Get straight A's.
2. Stop biting my nails.
3. Go to Stanford on a soccer scholarship.

Having earned the A's needed to get into the academically challenging school, Julie followed her dream and entered Stanford University. For the first three years the Foudy family paid full tuition. In her senior year the university awarded Julie Foudy a soccer scholarship, the first offered to a soccer player.

What about her resolution to stop biting her fingernails? Julie examines the stubby cuticles and shrugs her shoulders. "Two out of three ain't bad!"

ON THE FIELD

As central midfielder Julie's job is to make plays happen. She compares it to the role of point guard in basketball or quarterback in football. Stationed between forwards and defenders, Julie directs traffic, blunting opponents' efforts before they become serious threats. "The idea is to link the team together," says Julie. Under constant pressure she shifts through chaos, always looking to deliver the perfect pass she hopes will result in a goal.

She became the co-captain of the National Team soon after the 1991 FIFA Women's World Cup. Why did the coaching staff think this twenty-year-old could handle the job? They recognized the obvious. Julie Foudy is very smart. Her communication style is direct and clear. She is the kind of player who expects no more than she's willing to give.

WNT captains Julie Foudy and Carla Overbeck's devotion to the team colors every decision they make. In the early years those decisions mainly focused on the playing field. But with each victory came greater visibility and more opportunity. Now their decisions include endorsements, contracts, and media issues. Julie explains, "When April Heinrichs [former WNT captain] handed us this team, she handed over an amazing team that had reached its highest level under her leadership. Our continued success has brought dividends which allow us to live as professional athletes. In the early years, many WNT players worked side jobs just to make ends meet. Sure, it's more complicated now, but our job is to bring this team to the next level, and that's what we're committed to do."

Best game moment: The Olympic semifinal match against Norway was her best soccer playing moment. With a score of 1–1, the game went into sudden death—the first team to score, won. Julie received the ball on the right, almost at the midfield. Says Julie, "I remember cutting inside, and instead of players coming at me, everything opened up, like the sea had parted. I kept dribbling. Finally their last defender stepped up, and that's when I saw Mac make that run. It was like slo-mo. Everything went blurry. I remember her running, and all I kept saying to myself was Don't hit it too hard, don't hit it too hard."

She didn't. Shannon MacMillan scored the golden goal, and the stadium erupted. Julie smiles; "We collapsed in a pile, our coaches, team doctors, everyone. After getting beat by them in the semifinals of the '95 Cup, beating them back in the Olympics was just so sweet."

Red card: During a game played in Brazil, as she lay on the field, a Brazilian player stomped on her very bruised leg for no good reason. Quite naturally, she reacted like anyone would. Julie offers a sly smile, "It hurt, so I kicked her off me. Of course, the ref only saw my kick, so he tossed me out."

Superstitions/lucky clothing/rituals: Before the 1995 Women's World Cup, Julie had to wear a certain pair of shorts before each game. When they lost to Norway, she burned them. "I stay away from superstitions now."

In the zone: Playing in the zone is a feeling of complete confidence. Says Julie, "Everything feels right without thinking about it."

Injuries: Julie Foudy credits genetics with her injury-free career. "I'm blessed. Ma and Pa gave me good bones and joints."

Jersey number: She has worn the number 11 since club soccer. Why 11? "When I was little,

I always wanted to be number one until I figured out that eleven was two number ones—even better!"

Blooper: The blooper happened in college, Stanford against Harvard, an annual game that always drew fans. The Stanford Cardinals were on Harvard's home field, huddled, minutes before game time when Julie felt nature call. As she was jogging back to the Stanford huddle, a soccer ball rolled in her path. She kicked it. Somehow, her feet tangled up and splat! She hit the ground hard. She dusted her embarrassed self off and heard the fans begin to clap slowly. By the time she reached the huddle, their claps had turned into applause. Julie smiles, "I remembered thinking, 'This is a good impression. I've really intimidated them now.'"

SOCCER IS MY LIFE

The first moment she stepped out on a field with Mia Hamm, Kristine Lilly, Carla Overbeck, Linda Hamilton, and Joy Biefeld (Fawcett), Julie Foudy met her kindred spirits. The young teenagers shared her passion. She could tell by the way they played. Says Julie,

"They were as competitive as I was, and no one apologized for it."

Another moment illuminating the importance of the game in her life came in the spring of 1989. Already on the WNT two years, Julie was close to becoming a starting player, but she needed to secure her position. The opportunity came during a tournament in Sardinia, Italy. There was only one problem. The tournament coincided with high school graduation. She had already missed her senior prom. Julie didn't want to miss graduation, nor did she want to send a message that the team wasn't important. The decision was difficult to make, but she went to Italy. Looking back, was it the right decision? Julie answers slowly. "The tournament was a turning point, I won my starting position, so from that perspective, it was the right decision to make."

But missing her high school commencement will always be a sore spot. Julie still can't listen to graduation stories. "When people start, I'm like, don't go there!"

ON INSPIRATION

Knowing the WNT offers inspiration to young athletes pleases Julie Foudy. She hopes girls, in particular, are inspired to play hard. Says Julie, "Playing competitively is really tough for some girls, especially if their friends are playing on the other team. They don't want to go after them."

Addressing that gender-specific trait is something Julie does in a soccer camp she holds each summer in Orange County, California. The girls-only camp offers traditional learning with an emphasis on skills and technique. It also emphasizes competition. She explains, "We help the girls connect to their competitive edge. I'm not talking about that sick, obsessed win-at-all-costs craziness. I'm talking about always playing to win. After the game you can hug and kiss and say you're sorry to your friends, but when you're on the field, you don't let yourself get beat for any reason."

Off the field Julie Foudy inspires, too. In 1997 she made global headlines by visiting a Reebok manufacturing plant in Pakistan. Child labor was an acceptable practice in that country but unacceptable to Julie Foudy. Her trip triggered reform. Today no child under the age of fifteen can stitch soccer balls. Says Julie, "Reebok has made positive changes, and that makes other companies change as well."

ADVICE TO YOUNG ATHLETES

Her advice is simple: go after your dream. The woman speaks from experience. Growing up, Julie Foudy had two dreams—one, play soccer at Stanford; two, become a sports announcer.

Her first dream came true right on schedule. The second one had to wait. For reasons she still can't explain, Julie believed becoming a sports announcer was unreachable. In college she majored in pre-med, a logical choice based on her love for science and math. Says Julie, "I got it in my head that becoming a doctor was realistic, but becoming a sports announcer wasn't."

But the dream wouldn't die, not even after she was accepted to Stanford Medical School. Julie decided to postpone medical school admission until after the 1995 Women's World Cup and the 1996 Olympic Games. By then she knew practicing medicine was not her calling.

Her second dream came true in the summer of 1998, when Julie Foudy sat in an ESPN anchor chair for one month and announced the FIFA Men's World Cup. Once the assignment was over, teammates sighed in relief. Why? For two months prior to Cup, when

Julie wasn't sequestered in the hotel room honing up on soccer history and facts, she was coercing teammates into playing her soccer version of *Trivial Pursuit*. She smiles. "I kinda drove them nuts."

Her debut on ESPN received glowing reviews. Julie Foudy knows her stuff, and on camera appears quite comfortable—a surprise to no one on the Women's National Team.

FACTS

Caps: 138

Goals: 27

Assists: 31

Sponsors: Reebok.

Causes: Child labor causes.

Coaching/camps: The Julie Foudy Girls Soccer Camp, summer annual held in Orange County, California.

Awards (partial list): 1991 FIFA World Cup winner; 1995 FIFA Women's World Cup Bronze Medal; 1996 Olympic Gold Medal; 1997 FIFA Fair Player

Humanitarian Service Award;
1997–present, contributing editor,
Women's Sports & Fitness magazine;
1998 Goodwill Games Gold Medal.

FAVORITES

Foods: Doughnuts, cereal, Indian and Thai.

Hobbies: Painting pottery, beach volleyball, golf, "killing my plants and cooking cereal for dinner."

Movies: "Deep movies like *Austin Powers, Happy Gilmore, My Cousin Vinnie!*"

Movie stars: Richard Gere, George Clooney.

TV shows: *Saturday Night Live, David Letterman, ER.*

$\star$ $\star$ $\star$

Mia Hamm

PERSONAL STATS

Position: Forward
Height: 5'5"
Weight: 125
Birthday: 3/17/72

SOCCER TEAMS

1985–1989 Lake Braddock Secondary School, Virginia, and Notre Dame High School Varsity Team, Texas

1987–present U.S. WNT

*L*ong time WNT trainer and self-professed *mother hen, Sue Hammond likes to tell the*

story about Mia Hamm's tastebuds. She likes her Gatorade on the sweet side. Each morning before training sessions begin, Sue makes gallons of the thirst quencher. One day she scrambled up proportions that turned the team's favorite, lemon-lime, into a lip-smacking tart brew. The next day she concocted another tart-tasting batch. On the third morning Mia Hamm knocked on the training room door early. Was the Gatorade made yet, she wanted to know. When Sue said no, Mia offered to taste-test a batch. She's been the team's official Gatorade taster ever since.

IN THE BEGINNING

Mia Hamm is now the third oldest in a family of five, but in her heart she will always be the fourth of six children. Her older brother Garrett died in 1997. The loss was hard on Mia. They were very close. He taught her many things. How to play soccer was one. Cameras often capture a wistful-looking Mia Hamm. When Garrett's name is mentioned, that wistfulness shadows her face, but then it's gone, replaced by a grin. He always made her smile, one reason she adored him.

The Hamms are a military family. Relocation is a way of life. During her young years, Mia lived in seven states. A slight drawl is left over from living many years in Texas towns. She also lived in Italy, where her dad, Colonel Bill Hamm, fell in love with European *futbol*, soccer. Once the Hamms returned to the states, Colonel Hamm found soccer teams for his older children. Soon he became their coach.

For shy children, relocating is harder than for those who can depend on the gift of gab to ease them into new environments. Sports became Mia's language, her way to fit in. Says Mia, "Competing was a common denominator. I'd join a team and make friends that way. Sports gave me confidence. I knew I could do it well."

Her movements are fluid and graceful, as if she's performing some kind of athletic ballet through a field of opponents scrambling to stop her. Her grace comes naturally. Stephanie Hamm, her mom, was a professional ballet dancer who retired from the stage when children came, but she never retired from dance. Each time they relocated, like Mia, Stephanie Hamm searched out those who shared her passion, other ballet dancers.

Mariel Margaret was the Hamm's third

daughter. Her mom nicknamed her Mia after a ballerina with whom she once studied. Ironically, ballet helped Mia choose soccer. Every Saturday morning her mom went to the ballet studio. The younger Hamms had a choice: go to the studio with Mom or follow Dad to the soccer fields. There was no contest. Soccer always won. Though Mia tried ballet, it didn't suit her. Team sports did.

She joined her first soccer team when they lived in Wichita Falls, Texas. Soccer wasn't big in Wichita Falls. When time came to advance, there were no girls teams to join, so Mia joined a boys team. She played with them until her family packed up and moved again, this time to San Antonio, Texas, where Mia joined a girls team.

By then Mia Hamm was getting noticed. She was invited to join the Olympic Development Program. There she met the players who would become her teammates and dear friends: Kristine Lilly, Julie Foudy, Carla Overbeck, and Joy Biefeld (Fawcett). She was thirteen years old.

At age fourteen the family moved again, this time back to Wichita Falls, where soccer had by then caught on. Mia joined a girls team. The buzz continued to build. At an ODP camp in New Orleans, a coach recognized her specialness and called his good friend, Anson Dorrance. The year was 1986. Dorrance, who had just formed the Women's National Team in 1985, agreed to watch Mia play at an ODP tournament, but he wasn't holding his breath. By then he had been coaching women's soccer at the University of North Carolina at Chapel Hill for seven years. Often, he heard people talk about phenomenal players. Rarely did they live up to their buildup. Mia Hamm proved the exception. When he watched the fifteen-year-old receive a pass and accelerate like she was shot from a cannon, Dorrance knew he was looking at a superstar in the making.

She joined the Under-19 National Team, played in a tournament, did well, and along with Foudy, Biefeld (Fawcett), Lilly, Hamilton, and Overbeck, was asked to join the WNT for a tournament in China. They did well there, too. Upon their return, the WNT coaching staff surprised many by cleaning house to make room for "the kids"—Anson Dorrance's nickname for this group of promising young players. The year was 1987. Mia Hamm was a high school sophomore.

Mia attended the University of North

Carolina and majored in political science. WNT teammate Kristine Lilly entered the same year. In their time there, the Tar Heels won four NCAA championships. During college, Mia met her future husband, Christiaan Corry. They took a Russian history course together and discovered many shared interests including their appreciation for military life. Corry is in the Marine Corps. They married in 1994. So far, his orders have relocated them to Florida and California. Not surprisingly, he reminds Mia of her dad. Lieutenant Christiaan Corry flies helicopters. Colonel Bill Hamm was a fighter pilot who served in Vietnam. Mia smiles. "Christiaan is a lot like my dad. They're both really great guys."

ON THE FIELD

Mia Hamm could have followed in her mother's footsteps and become a ballet dancer. She practically pirouettes through opponents with a speed and gracefulness any ballet dancer would admire—petite and delicate, a ballerina hell-bent on scoring. As a forward, her main responsibility is to score and set up players to score. Forwards are sometimes called glory hounds. The name does not apply to Mia Hamm. When she scores, there are no theatrics, no falling to her knees, no dance, just Mia running toward her teammates, usually with head bowed, inspiring one writer to make this comparison: it's as if she's surveying the crowd through a periscope in her ponytail.

She has been called the best female soccer player in the world, an assessment WNT coach Tony DiCicco says is accurate when Mia Hamm is on her game. That's for him to say, not her. Mia considers herself no better than any other player on the team. But the more she insists this is true, the more her fans insist otherwise.

Numbers don't lie. Her numbers are staggering. In a game played in the fall of 1998, Mia Hamm scored her hundredth goal. No soccer player—female or male—in U.S. history has ever scored more. The closest player to her, Michelle Akers, may still catch up, but for now, Mia Hamm is the front runner. The placement suits her.

Best game moment: The undisputed best moment of her soccer-playing career happened after the WNT won the final game and stood on the Olympic podium to receive gold medals. Says Mia, "It was such a privilege to be there next to my sixteen best friends. The fact that my family was there made it more perfect." As the National Anthem played, the six-game series reran in her head. Says Mia, "Players who were only called upon for fifteen minutes came out and gave it everything they had. Our sense of pride was enormous."

Red card: None.

Superstitions/lucky clothing/rituals: Mia Hamm showers before every game. She also drinks lots of water. Says Mia, "I worry about becoming dehydrated, especially if it's hot."

In the zone: Mia describes playing in the zone this way. "When I'm playing my best, I don't have to think about doing anything. It just comes to me. I'm glad I don't think about it 'cause I'd probably mess up if I did!"

Injuries: She knocks wood. "None."

Jersey number: When she joined WNT in 1987, Mia was the youngest player picked, therefore she received the only number remaining, 9.

Blooper: "I trip a lot," Mia offers matter-of-factly. Yeah, sure. "Really, I'm not kidding. There's been several times when I've gone to kick the ball and tripped myself." One time the ref even blew his whistle. She explains, "I'd kicked the ball hard, missed it, and landed right on my butt. I'm sure he thought I couldn't have done it alone, someone must have pushed me, but no one did."

SOCCER IS MY LIFE

"Making the national team was the pivotal point in my life," Mia Hamm says. Though playing next to Michelle Akers and April Heinrichs intimidated her, her first WNT tournament was a confidence booster. Says Mia, "I had a little taste of success in that tournament. Enough for me to say, 'You can do this.'"

On the WNT Mia found her soulmates, players who viewed the game as she did. Says Mia, "Here I was, surrounded by people who were totally intense about what they were doing. People who worked as hard as I did but also had fun. I just wanted to continue to be a part of that."

The name Hamm has always invited one-liners like, Is Mia Hamm a ham? In public, she definitely isn't. Her shyness is almost legendary. But when she's with teammates, her shyness evaporates. With them another side of Mia emerges, and yes, this one is a bit of a ham.

During the 1998 Goodwill Games, Mia took a van ride into Manhattan with Julie Foudy, Brandi Chastain, Kristine Lilly, and Carla Overbeck to promote the 1999 Women's World Cup at a press luncheon. During the drive in, the group chatted while they noshed on food— lots of it, including Fig Newtons, pretzels, Fritos, and a Powerbar or two. The topic of celebrity came up. Mia was asked how she handles the frenzy that often surrounds her. Sitting close by was Julie Foudy. Mia pushed Julie's shoulder and grinned, "I just try to pick up Julie's scraps every now and then." When Julie shot her the evil eye, Mia added, "You know, whatever leftovers I can get. Right, Juls?"

In the company of her girlfriends, Mia is not shy or wary, she's the girl they've known since she was thirteen years old. A girl who likes to sing. Many WNT players do. On bus trips, several will spontaneously burst into song. Some sing off-key. Mia Hamm can hold a note.

She doesn't know what the future holds

beyond the year 2000. Her continued playing depends on the development of a women's soccer league. The fact that the U.S. has not formed a professional league concerns her. A professional league is critical to the development of female soccer players in this country. The problem no longer is finding good players—colleges are full of them—the problem is where to play after graduation. "When you graduate from college, you have to make decisions about your future. You can't play soccer at a competitive level, improve, and hold down a full-time job, too. It's impossible," Mia says, "and there are only so many spots on the National Team." Many players relocate to countries like Japan in order to play competitive league soccer. Says Mia, "If we want to stay on top, we have to put a league together so players can play full-time. Otherwise, we're going to lose our lead. It's that simple, really."

ON INSPIRATION

Growing up, Mia admired several athletes including Wayne Gretzky and Jackie Joyner-Kersee, but she never felt inspired by them. Her inspiration came from her family. Her brother Garrett, especially.

One of two children adopted by the Hamms, Garrett was three years older than Mia. At age seventeen, he was diagnosed with a rare blood disorder, aplastic anemia. For many years he battled the painful disease gallantly.

Garrett Hamm's athletic talents inspired his younger sister to excel. His soccer team always brought home the biggest trophies. Says Mia, "I wanted one so bad. That's all I could think about. How was I gonna get a big trophy like Garrett's?"

Inspiring young girls pleases Mia Hamm. "By being here, we offer another choice, a choice we didn't have growing up. Now girls can say, 'I want to be a nurse, I want to be a doctor, or I want to be a professional soccer player.' I like that."

Her shyness as a little girl sometimes made Mia feel less than confident. If she offers inspiration to children, Mia Hamm gives the impression she hopes the ones who struggle with shyness get an extra dose.

ADVICE TO YOUNG ATHLETES

Mia is the name fans scream most. Her record-breaking number of goals is one reason. Her eagle-in-flight runs down the field, another. She has adjusted to the extra attention. She likes being surrounded by young fans, but she isn't fond of pushy parents. It upsets her to see parents nudging their children toward her. Mia knows how hard it is for some kids to say hi or ask for an autograph. She wouldn't like being pushed. She bets they don't, either. Says Mia, "The advice I always give kids is to make sure you're playing soccer because you love it, not because your parents do."

She also hopes young players enjoy the game. "Not everyone is going to play in the Olympics or be on the National Team. Not everyone will play ODP. The important thing, the only thing that matters, is to enjoy playing. It's a game. The level you reach is secondary. If it's recreational, club, varsity, or whatever, have fun. Otherwise, what's the point?"

Young players should take the time to enjoy their accomplishments on the field. Says Mia, "I think it's a problem with girls, especially. We aren't taught to celebrate our successes like boys are." Mia smiles and says, "It's a good thing to say 'nice job' and pat yourself on the back once in a while.'"

She tries to practice what she preaches. "I'm so intense, I don't enjoy things as much as I could. I'm trying to learn how to relax more, too."

★　　★　　★

FACTS

Caps: 157

Goals: 101

Assists: 76

Sponsors: Nike, Gatorade, Powerbar, Mattel, Earthgrains.

Causes: Bone Marrow Foundation; Smoke-Free Kids, a soccer anti-smoking campaign.

Coaching/camps: Kristine Lilly Soccer Academy coach, Julie Foudy Soccer Camp, UNC soccer camps.

Awards (partial list): 3-time NSCAA All-American; 2-time Missouri Athletic Club and Hermann Award winner; 1991 FIFA World Cup Gold Medal; 1994–95 Honda Broderick Award winner; 1995 FIFA World Cup Bronze Medal; 1996 Olympic Gold Medal; 1998 Goodwill Games Gold Medal.

FAVORITES

Food: Italian, Thai.
Hobbies: Golf, reading, cooking.
Movies: *When Harry Met Sally.*
Movie stars: John Malkovich.
TV shows: *ER.*

★ ★ ★

Kristine Lilly

PERSONAL STATS

Position: Midfielder
Height: 5'4"
Weight: 120
Birthday: 7/22/71

SOCCER TEAMS

1978–1985 Wilton Wonders, Boys Traveling
Team
1985–1989 Wilton High School Varsity Soccer
Team
1989–1992 University of North Carolina Tar
Heels

1994–present Tyreso Football Club, Sweden
1987–present U.S. WNT

*K*ristine Lilly signed up for an after-dinner
All-American Girls *interview but canceled
a few hours later. After a hard day training for
the 1998 Goodwill Games, it was understand-
able. She was tired, no doubt. "Oh, no!"
exclaimed Kristine. "It's just that there's a great
mall nearby and tonight's the only night I can
shop. How about afterward?"*

*At 9:30 P.M. Kristine sat down for her inter-
view wearing a satisfied smile. "I caught some
great sales!"*

IN THE BEGINNING

When Kristine Lilly was asked to recall her
earliest soccer memories, she immediately
replied, "Oranges! I remember our moms
passing them out at halftime. I lived for those
wedges!" She also remembers the color of her
first jersey. It was baby blue with a soccer
association patch on the left shoulder. Did she
love the game from the start? She sounds surprised the question would even be asked.
"Absolutely. On game day I'd get up really
early, put on my uniform, and sit there wait-

ing. If we got rained out, I would cry, that's how much I loved it."

Even at the age of six, teammates depended on her to score, a talent nurtured by her grandmother. Says Kristine, "She gave me twenty-five cents for every goal. I would put them in this jar. Gosh, I wish I still had that jar today." By now it would be brimming over. Her grandma's incentive went up to a dollar per goal once Kristine made the Women's National Team.

But soccer wasn't her only love. Baseball ran a close second. For several years Kristine played both. Her hometown, Wilton, Connecticut, offered more opportunities for boys to play organized sports than for girls, so from second through eighth grade, she played on boys teams. Playing with boys taught her how to be tough. Her older brother Scott delivered the first lesson. Kristine smiles. "He would never give me an inch. I earned everything I got when I competed against him."

When she began playing soccer in the late 1970s, club teams didn't exist in her area. Players with promise graduated to traveling leagues. She joined one, the Wilton Wonders, and played with them for the next six years.

They won several state championships, which qualified them for regional competition. She recalls one competition vividly. Says Kristine, "This big guy was marking me. He towered over me. Everywhere I went, there he was, breathing down my neck. I remember making this quick turn"—she pauses, her face turns pink—"I, ah, as I turned, my elbow rammed him in not a very good place." What happened next? "The poor guy buckled over in pain. The crowd started to roar, I mean really laugh loud." Kristine then did what she was raised to do. "I immediately said, 'I am so sorry.'"

In the mid-1980s Kristine Lilly was discovered by national team coaches who invited her to the U-19 National Team training camp. She didn't want to go. Says Kristine, "I'm kind of a homebody. I just didn't want to be away that long." Fortunately, her parents nudged her to go. There she met Mia Hamm, Julie Foudy, Carla Overbeck, Joy Fawcett, and Linda Hamilton (retired WNT player), young players who became her good buddies instantly. By the end of training camp, they all made the U-19 National Team and immediately played in a tournament. They did so well, WNT coaches invited them to join the national team for a tournament in China. Again, Kristine was reluctant to go. She hadn't been home for weeks and China was far away, so instead of saying yes immediately, she told WNT head coach Anson Dorrance she'd have to ask her parents for permission. After all, she was only sixteen.

Kristine approached the China trip with a certain amount of apprehension. Teammate Julie Foudy still teases her about the raggedy old stuffed tiger she brought on the trip. Kristine says, "His name was Tamba. I couldn't sleep without him."

ON THE FIELD

Kristine Lilly smiles. "On a good day they call me Lil!"

Midfield players constantly run to cover space; therefore, being in top physical condition is essential. Kristine calls herself a leader who has a workhorse mentality and knows how to finish a play. Her sixty-one goals speak to that fact. One of the team's playmakers, Kristine either defends against assault or initiates the forward attack. She also calls herself a patient player. Says Kristine, "When you play outside midfield, the ball isn't always coming at you, so there's time to daydream. At this level you'd better not."

Described as the fittest WNT player, Kristine Lilly's fitness routine doesn't alter much during off-season. Part of her daily workout includes a three-mile run on stairs. She also does a drill called Suicide Test which employs five cones set at intervals through which she sprints in under thirty-five seconds. After a twenty-five second rest, she repeats it ten times. A drill called Stinkers employs cones at forty-yard intervals through which she sprints in under fifty seconds. After a forty-second rest she repeats it six to ten times. For each cone missed Kristine adds another repetition. In spite of her daily rigorous training schedule, Kristine does not consider herself the fittest WNT player. Says Kristine, "Carla [Overbeck] is the fittest. She inspires me."

A player who puts her heart into every game, Kristine sometimes is so physically and mentally exhausted at the end of a game that her tears flow easily. She remembers one high school game that triggered a flood. It was a state championship game and the crowd was hostile, especially to her. Hecklers screamed, "Lilly you stink!" all game long. Her team lost.

Afterward, Kristine sat on the bench crying when two teenage boys approached her. They were from the other side, so she braced herself for more abuse. Instead, they apologized, then said she was a great player. Says Kristine, "That erased everything else that happened. Not because they complimented me, but because their words told me they understood this game and my love for it. To this day, that's the most amazing thing that's ever happened to me on a soccer field."

Best game moment: Her best moment happened after the WNT won the inaugural FIFA Women's World Cup in 1991. The games were held in China. Once the national team collected medals and sang the National Anthem, they walked off the field past bleachers filled with American players' families. She spotted her dad. Says Kristine, "I'll just never forget the way he looked at me that day. There he was, wearing his red jacket with an American flag sticker on his cheek. I'd never seen him smile the way he smiled at me that day. His eyes were full of tears. That just captured it all for me."

Red card: None.

Superstitions/lucky clothing/rituals: Before games she's faithful to a specific routine. First, while still in the locker room, she pulls her hair back into a ponytail. She saves this for last because ponytails trigger headaches. Then, right before leaving for the field, Kristine removes her boyfriend's necklace. Once on the field Kristine does three jump headers before the whistle blows—not two, not four, but three.

In the zone: When Kristine Lilly is in the zone, she doesn't second-guess herself. Says Kristine, "When I get the ball, I know exactly what I'm going to do. It's total confidence. I love the feeling!"

Injuries: Kristine knocks wood. "So far, none."

Jersey number: The number 13 had no special significance when she was assigned it—now she loves it.

Blooper: Several moments on the field have turned Kristine's face red, but the most embarrassing one happened off the field. Kristine was asked to address students and faculty at her alma mater, UNC, about what it takes to be a premiere athlete. On stage were several other speakers. UNC's men's basketball coach Dean Smith officiated. Though she graduated with a degree in communications, talking in front of large groups has never come easy for Kristine. She stood there with cue cards in hand and began to sweat profusely. Suddenly the room went black and she fainted. Dean Smith broke her fall. As she was helped off stage, the crowd gave her a standing ovation. For days she was flooded with kind notes. The one written by Dean Smith remains her favorite. Says Kristine, "He thanked me for doing such a great job for my school and told me he didn't particularly like speaking in front of large crowds, either." Since then, Kristine has taken instruction in public speaking. She now enjoys speaking to large groups. Taking a lesson from her approach to soccer, Kristine no longer uses cue cards. "Now I just speak from my heart."

SOCCER IS MY LIFE

Kristine attended the University of North Carolina at Chapel Hill. With academics and soccer there was no time left for other sports. For a consummate athlete, one who loves to play many sports, this realization produced a bittersweet moment.

Sports have never been just about excelling in a game. For someone more comfortable listening than talking, playing sports provided an outlet for her emotions. Kristine explains, "I'm not one to open up. When things really bother me, I hold them inside." Until she gets on the soccer field. In the game Kristine gets noisy, shouting commands, delivering pep talks, and even crying when tears are needed. The ability to express emotions on the field has helped her through some personally tough times. Right before college her parents told her they were getting divorced. Kristine says, "I was shocked. For the longest time I kept everything locked inside. The only place I expressed my feelings was in the game. I think that's a big reason why I played so well during my college years. I had this pain inside that spilled out on the field."

It's common for children of divorce to fantasize about parents reuniting. College student Kristine was no exception. Says Kristine, "At my games they sat together and cheered me on. Afterward we'd always go out as a family, so I figured maybe they'd get back together."

She has now reconciled with her parents'

new lives. Both are happy. Says Kristine, "I know they both love me very much. I can't ask for more."

ON INSPIRATION

Growing up, Kristine's brother Scott inspired her most. Why? Kristine explains, "'Cause I always wanted to beat him!" Their relationship thrived on competition. If she tried to fake an injury, Scott wasn't buying. His tough love made her excel. Says Kristine, "I could be on the field screaming, and Scott'd say, 'She's okay.'"

Many WNT teammates name Kristine Lilly as the player who inspires them. For Kristine, Carla Overbeck and Joy Fawcett offer inspiration. Giving birth and returning to the game is the reason. Says Kristine, "They both left the game as the greatest defenders in the world. When they returned, they had to climb back up again. I watched how they did whatever was needed to regain their skills and confidence. They've made our whole team see things so much differently. Now we all want kids!" Offering inspiration to young players is one reason why Kristine Lilly runs a summer soccer camp in Wilton, Connecticut. Teammates

Mia Hamm, Julie Foudy, Tisha Venturini, Joy Fawcett, and Shannon MacMillan help coach. Says Kristine, "The camp helps us deliver the message that we're human, just like them. Afterward, when I see my campers in town, they come up to me and instead of asking for my autograph, they just say hi and start talking about whatever. When kids can connect on a personal level, they're more likely to believe they can do it, too. I feel really good about that. We all do."

ADVICE TO YOUNG ATHLETES

Kristine Lilly advises children to compete. Says Kristine, "Competing helps you develop everything you need to survive. Your heart, your desire, your toughness, everything essential. Competing makes you know what you're made of."

For girls especially, Kristine advises competitive sports. She explains. "Girls are so often given messages that they can't do things as well as boys. Competing erases all that junk." Serious young soccer players must be serious about fitness. Says Kristine, "The way I see it, you're given a God-given talent. Sure, you can practice to improve it, but there's only so much you can do. The talent you've been given is not in your control. Being in the best possible shape to maximize your talent is in your control. That's why I take such pride in being fit. When you come to the game prepared and you play with your heart, no one can expect more. Even if you lose, you will be respected for the contributions you make to the team."

FACTS

Caps: 163, the most capped soccer player in the world

Goals: 61

Assists: 52

Sponsors: Adidas.

Causes: Smoke-Free Kids, a soccer anti-smoking campaign; World Wildlife Fund.

Coaching/camps: The Kristine Lilly Soccer Academy, 41 Scribner Hill, Wilton, CT 06897.

Awards (partial list): 4-time NCAA National Championship, UNC; 1991 FIFA World

Cup winner; 1993 USSF Player of the
Year; 1996 Olympic Gold Medal.

FAVORITES

Food: Grandma's apple pie, Mom's double
stuffed potatoes, and Dad's Christmas
morning breakfast which includes eggs
over easy.

Hobbies: Listening to music—Nancy Griffith,
R.E.M., The Indigo Girls; Rollerblading;
photography, especially sunsets.

Movies: *Stripes*.

Movie stars: Julia Roberts, Michelle Pfeiffer,
Johnny Depp, Tom Hanks, Meg Ryan,
Anthony Hopkins, Harrison Ford.

TV shows: *Friends*, *Party of Five*.

★ ★ ★

Shannon MacMillan

PERSONAL STATS

Position: Forward/Midfielder
Height: 5'4½"
Weight: 130
Birthday: 10/7/74

SOCCER TEAMS

**1979–1985 AYSO Community Soccer
Teams, Shooting Starlets, Chicklets,
Rosebuds**
**1989–1992 San Pasqual High School Golden
Eagles**
**1988–1992 Rancho Bernardo Hornets
(changed to La Jolla Nomads)**

1992–1995 University of Portland Pilots
1996–1997 Shiroki Serena (Japan League)
1993–present U.S. WNT

S occer players love to embarrass opponents by kicking the ball between their legs. It's called nutmegging, a Shannon MacMillan favorite.

One day she and Julie Foudy decided to spice up their practice with this challenge: who could nutmeg more? They had so much fun, they carried the contest over to the next day's game, which WNT lost 4–1. Coach DiCicco was not happy. Nor was Shannon or Julie. Neither one had successfully executed one nutmeg. The next day the team watched the game on tape. DiCicco spotted Julie's maneuver, stopped the tape, and lambasted her. She admitted wrongdoing but kept quiet about Shannon. The tape continued until Shannon's attempted nutmeg appeared on screen. Again, Coach DiCicco stopped the tape. "What the x!?*@?! were you doing, Mac? A surgeon couldn't have gotten that pass through there!"

Since Julie hadn't tattled, Shannon could have blamed the maneuver on poor judgment, but she couldn't let her friend take the rap alone. "I was going for the meg, too!" she exclaimed. Everyone started laughing, even Tony DiCicco.

IN THE BEGINNING

Shannon MacMillan began playing community soccer, a game she called "bumblebee ball" at age five. Says Shannon, "We'd swarm up and down the field with no real instruction but lots of support from the sidelines."

In sixth grade the MacMillans moved from California to Long Island, New York. For the next two years she played with a traveling team, an experience that offered her her first taste of competitive soccer. When she moved back to southern California, Shannon found a club team, and for the next four years played on the Rancho Bernardo Hornets (later known as the La Jolla Nomads).

The Hornets taught her how to be a team player. It was a lesson hard learned. Says Shannon, "When I was in Long Island, I was fast so they put me up front. I played no defense, I just scored, so when I joined the Hornets, I parked up front and waited for them to pass me the ball."

Her teammates had other ideas. They expected her to contribute more than just goals. Shannon was close to quitting when she realized something: they were right. She needed to round out her game to help the team more. In no time, she did.

The Hornets rose through the ranks. By sophomore year Shannon felt so sure of her soccer-playing abilities that she set this goal: to someday play soccer in the Olympics. Says Shannon, "I was at my best friend Steph's house having dinner, and I told her parents, 'I'm gonna play soccer in the Olympics.' I was so stoked about it, they didn't have the heart to tell me women's soccer wasn't even in the Olympics back then."

She played other sports in high school including softball, basketball, and track, but her heart belonged to soccer. Her club team won state and regional titles and an invitation to the national championship. Shannon had several college offers to play soccer. She chose the University of Portland because Clive Charles was there. He was a top-ranked soccer coach, but that's not why she chose his program. Says Shannon, "He's the most decent man you'll ever meet. Playing for him was a privilege."

The road to the national team was bumpy. She almost made it once, but a case of

The 1996 gold medal–winning U.S. Olympic Team

Kristine Lilly and Julie Foudy at the Olympics
PHOTO COURTESY OF KRISTINE LILLY

Kristine, age 9
PHOTO COURTESY OF KRISTINE LILLY

Julie as a child
PHOTO COURTESY OF JULIE FOUDY

Mia Hamm, age 6
PHOTO COURTESY OF MIA HAMM

Mia at the Olympic Gold Medal Ceremony in 1996
PHOTO COURTESY OF MIA HAMM

Joy Fawcett as a child
PHOTO COURTESY OF JOY FAWCETT

Stars like Joy and Shannon MacMillan inspire a
new generation of soccer players.
PHOTO BY MARLA MILLER

Cindy Parlow played for the storied UNC Tar Heels.
PHOTO BY OLLIE BROCK

Cindy got an early start on her ball-handling skills.
PHOTO COURTESY OF CINDY PARLOW

Tisha Venturini,
age 6

Mia Hamm and Tisha taking a break

Briana Scurry tending goal
PHOTO COURTESY OF BRIANA SCURRY

Briana, age 13
PHOTO COURTESY OF
BRIANA SCURRY

Shannon MacMillan,
age 5
PHOTO COURTESY OF
SHANNON MACMILLAN

Brandi Chastain, age 12
PHOTO COURTESY OF ROGER CHASTAIN

Shannon and Brandi at the 1996 Olympic Opening
Ceremonies   PHOTO COURTESY OF BRANDI CHASTAIN

Michelle Akers goes for the ball in a 1991 World
Cup Qualifier. PHOTO BY JOHN VAN WOERDEN

Michelle, age 8 PHOTO BY ANNE AKERS

Tiffany Roberts, age 8
PHOTO COURTESY OF TIFFANY ROBERTS

Tiffany with fans   PHOTO BY MARLA MILLER

Tiffeny Milbrett fights for the ball.
PHOTO COURTESY OF TIFFENY MILBRETT

Tiffeny *(far right)* as a child
PHOTO COURTESY OF TIFFENY MILBRETT

Carla Overbeck *(with ball)* on a youth team
PHOTO COURTESY OF CARLA OVERBECK

Kristine Lilly, Carin Gabarra, Carla, and Julie Foudy
PHOTO COURTESY OF JULIE FOUDY

Tracy Ducar makes a save in goal.
PHOTO BY STEVE SLADE

Tracy on the U-14 Massachusetts State Team
PHOTO COURTESY OF TRACY NOONAN DUCAR

Lorrie Fair with her twin sister, Ronnie
PHOTO COURTESY OF LORRAINE FAIR

Lorrie played under famed coach Anson Dorrance
at UNC.
PHOTO COURTESY OF LORRAINE FAIR

Christie Pearce

Christie, age 2, already working the ball

Julie Foudy

The WNT during a break from training for the 1999
World Cup

mononucleosis sidelined her. Then in 1993, during her college sophomore year, Shannon joined the WNT. Those early years she never felt secure. In the winter of 1996, six months before the Olympic Games, the team went into a training camp to determine who would move into residency, the six-month Olympic training camp. Shannon did not make the first cut.

She returned to Portland livid. The first person she visited was Clive Charles. Shannon says, "I was so mad. I called the coaching staff every name in the book. Soccer was my life. It got me everything I had. Now what was I going to do? I ranted and raved while Clive sat there listening."

A typical reaction for the British-born guru of soccer, who by then had become her dear friend. Finally he said, "Have a good wallow for the next twenty-four hours and then get back on the field. You're going to get another chance, and you've got to be ready when they call." What was her reply? She smiles. "I was like, yeah sure, Clive, what do you know?"

Enough, apparently. The WNT coaches did call her back. In the 1996 Olympic Games, Shannon MacMillan scored a total of three goals. In the last six minutes of the semi-final game against Norway, she scored the famous golden goal that put WNT in the finals, and the rest, as they say, is history.

ON THE FIELD

In 1993 Shannon joined the national team playing forward, a position she excelled at. In 1996 the coaching staff switched her to the midfield. Playing forward came naturally. "You've got freedom as a forward," says Shannon. "Technically, you're a goal-scoring machine."

Learning the midfield took time. Midfield players cover more space, assume more responsibility. Their job includes marking players who cause trouble while always trying to cause trouble back. Midfielders look for ways to support and set up the forwards to score. They also ease the workload on defenders and the goalkeeper by keeping players out of their space. Called the workhorses of the team, midfielders are always in motion and tend to be the fittest team players.

Kristine Lilly and Joy Fawcett helped her make the transition. Says Shannon, "Imagine two better teachers. Lil on one side of me showing me how it's done, and Joy behind me.

I'd hear her say, 'Don't worry, Mackie, I got you covered.' That's very comforting when you're out there learning. I've been very lucky."

She loves competition. At a pregame practice in Japan, she and Mia Hamm engaged in a little shooting match against Kristine Lilly and Brandi Chastain. Shannon laughs. "Mia and I were on fire. I bet we outshot them ten to two. Lil and Brandi were so mad. At the end, of course we had to rub it in. I go, 'Maybe tomorrow we'll come over there and take some left-footed shots.' Ooooh, that really made them mad!"

Competition continues off the field, too. Players spend hours playing board games. Her favorite partner is Joy Fawcett against Julie Foudy and Brandi Chastain. However, she admits that thirst for competition has caused problems in her personal life. "My roommates won't play board games with me 'cause I'm too intense. I know I have to work on that."

Best game moment: Her eyes still fill with tears when she remembers the semifinal game of the 1996 Olympics. Of the three goals she scored in the Olympic Games, the second one became her best moment. The game went into sudden death—the first team to score won.

Shannon says, "I remember right before going in, April [retired WNT captain–turned–coach], hits my head and says, 'We need you to win this, Mac.'" Shannon's first touch on the ball was unimpressive—it bounced off her shin—but April's words rang in her head. "I knew she believed in me. That helped a lot," she says.

Shannon doesn't remember the forty-yard run she made to get the ball from Julie. She only remembers Julie Foudy running. Says Shannon, "All of a sudden I see this gap open up, and I remember saying, 'Oh my gosh, I'm in.' Julie read it from miles away and hits this ball. Honest, I've never had such a perfect pass delivered to me. If it was any softer, Norway's defense would have swallowed it up. Any harder, their keeper would've grabbed it. Out of the corner of my eye I saw Norway's sweeper coming at me as I hit the ball with the inside of my foot and watched it roll in. All I could think of was 'Where's Julie, I've got to find that girl!'"

Red card: None.

Superstitions/lucky clothing/rituals: Shannon snaps a rubber band on her wrist and says, "Colleen Hacker, our sports psychologist, has me wear this. When I do something I don't like, I snap it." During games, she always wears her number 8 charm necklace.

In the zone: The only time Shannon played in the zone was during the Olympic semifinal game. "I don't remember the run I made, I only remember seeing Julie, and the next thing I knew, the team was piled on top of me."

Injuries: In 1995 Shannon required foot surgery for a Jones Fracture. She now has a titanium screw in her left foot. In 1997 a kneecap injury also required surgery in the middle of the WNT's season; she returned thirteen days later, which was a mistake. The knee became re-injured. "If I had to do it over again, I would have let myself heal properly."

Jersey number: When she joined WNT, the number 8 was the only available number. That was okay. "Eight was my very first jersey number. I think that's pretty cool."

Blooper: It's not her blooper but the embarrassing moment that still stings was when her club team played in the national championship game. Says Shannon, "We lost the final game by two. Our sweeper scored both goals." Both goals? She nods and laughs a little. "She felt just awful about it. The plane ride home was real quiet."

SOCCER IS MY LIFE

Shannon played several sports in high school. One day at track practice her coach criticized her for running with her elbows out. Says Shannon, "He said I ran like a soccer player. That's when it hit me hard—I was a soccer player. I quit track right then."

Playing soccer with her club team shaped her attitude about the game. They had a strong sense of team. When she joined them, she had been the goal-scoring machine, the star. By the time she left four years later, she had learned this lesson: the whole is greater than any one part.

At fourteen, Shannon and six club team-mates made the Olympic Development Program's district team. They were thrilled, but there was one problem. None of the girls could afford ODP fees. Saying no felt terrible until their coach, Tom Schwartz, came up with a plan. He told the girls if they gave him their commitment to practice daily for the entire summer, they could make something happen. Says Shannon, "I remember him saying, 'We don't need ODP. Just give me your commitment.'"

They did. That season the Hornets won State Cup, went on to regionals, won that, and went on to the national championship. They fought their way into the finals by overcoming a 2–0 lead in the semifinal game to win 3–2. Shannon scored all three goals. Though they lost the final game, the Hornets went home victorious.

Their victory drew attention from college coaches, who started calling. Says Shannon, "That's when I began to believe my club coach might be right, maybe I didn't need ODP." Her confidence strengthened with each phone call. When Anson Dorrance from the University of North Carolina called, Shannon had already committed to the University of Portland. She remembers Dorrance's response: "I guess I'm a day late and a dollar short," he'd said. Did a phone call from the man who put women's soccer on the national map tempt her to switch schools? No, it didn't. Says Shannon, "I was playing for Clive Charles, that's where I belonged, but it was great getting Anson's call."

Today Shannon has little time to do much besides train, play, and attend to personal matters, like paying bills, during her time off. She would like to meet a nice man. Says Shannon, "In fact, I just said that to my roommate, who said, 'Well, if you were home for more than two weeks straight, maybe you would!'"

There is a price to pay for being on the Women's National Team, but Shannon Mac-Millan is willing to pay it. "The way I look at it, I can't do this forever, so I'm going to do it for as long as I can. The rest will just fall into place."

ON INSPIRATION

Many people have offered Shannon MacMillan inspiration—her teammates, Coach Clive Charles—but at the top of her people-who-inspire-me list is her older brother, Sean. Says Shannon, "I've never had a lot of confidence. Sean's always been in my corner. We've been through a lot together."

Having a sister who played like Shannon sometimes posed problems for Sean. Shannon giggles like a little sister, "His buddies always wanted me on their team. Sometimes I'd date one, and that really drove him nuts!"

Because she didn't have female athletes to look up to when she was a child, Shannon is delighted young girls now look up to her and her teammates. "I know meeting us makes girls believe they can do it, too. I love seeing that in their faces. I really love it."

ADVICE TO YOUNG ATHLETES

Shannon MacMillan remembers the soccer coach in high school who told her she wouldn't last one week in Division I ball. Says Shannon, "I almost quit, but then I decided it would be more fun to hang around and prove him wrong. I always tell kids, believe in yourself even when other people don't."

More advice: play on a team. The lessons learned can be incorporated into life. It was teamwork that won the gold medal. She cites Tiffeny Milbrett's winning goal in the final game against China as the best example of teamwork at play. Joy Fawcett passed the ball that turned into the winning goal. Says Shannon, "If you look at the ball Joy passed, a lot of players, myself included, would have taken the shot themselves. She had about a sixty-forty chance of making it in, but being the consummate team player she is, Joy saw

Millie was wide open, so she passed it to increase our odds. That's the teamwork I'm talking about."

FACTS

Caps: 63

Goals: 14

Assists: 15

Sponsors: Adidas.

Coaching/camps: Assistant coach, University of Portland.

Awards (partial list): 4-time All-American; 1993–95 University of Portland MVP; 1995 Hermann Award, Missouri Athletic Club Award; Honda Award; 1996 Olympic Gold Medal; 1998 Goodwill Games Gold Medal.

FAVORITES

Foods: Mexican, German, Chinese.

Hobbies: Reading, shopping, hanging out
with friends, writing.

Movies: *Fried Green Tomatoes, A League of Their
Own, Top Gun, Grease, Far and Away.*

Movie stars: Michelle Pfeiffer, Tom Cruise.

TV shows: *Friends, ER.*

Tiffeny Milbrett

PERSONAL STATS

Position: Forward
Height: 5'2"
Weight: 132
Birthday: 10/23/72

SOCCER TEAMS

1981–1985 Two recreational and two local
club teams

1985–1987 F.C. Portland Soccer Club

1987–1990 Hillsboro High School Spartans

1988–1989 C.F.F.C. Portland Soccer Club

1990–1994 University of Portland, Pilots

1995–1997 FC Shiroki Serena

1991–present U.S. WNT

*T*iffeny Milbrett's kindness is best seen when she's around children. She likes them. They like her. One morning she was about to begin practice for the 1998 Goodwill Games when a little girl holding out a program asked for her autograph.

Tiffeny smiled. "You bet. What's your name?"

With eyes cast down, the girl answered, "Jessica."

Tiffeny looked down, too. "Those are good cleats you're wearing, Jessica."

"Yeah, they are," replied the little girl, her eyes still cast down.

"If we have time, we're gonna kick a few balls around after practice. Why don't you join us?"

Jessica's head bobbed up. "Okay, sure," she said, now all eyes and smiles.

Tiffeny signed the program, tapped it lightly on the little girl's head, and said, "See ya, Jess," then ran out to the field.

IN THE BEGINNING

At five feet two Tiffeny Milbrett is not tall. She isn't small, either. Muscles outlining her arms and legs define a sturdiness built to last. Her straight, blond-streaked hair is almost always tied up in a ponytail. She is quiet but not shy. When something's on her mind, she says it, a personality trait that inspired her college chums to nickname her No Tact Tiff. She smiles. "Some of it was pure innocence. When I thought something, I just said it."

Tiffeny grew up in Hillsboro, Oregon. Her roots are working class. Elsie Milbrett-Parham was a single parent who raised Tiffeny and her older brother, Mark, alone. Money was never plentiful.

Athleticism runs in the Milbrett gene pool. Her mom is an athlete who grew up in the 1950s in a small farming town that didn't offer girls sports. She learned by playing with her older brother. Tiffeny grew up watching her mom play softball and soccer. At fifty-something, Elsie Milbrett-Parham still plays in a soccer league.

Tiffeny joined her first soccer team at age eight. The uniforms were bright yellow and royal blue. Her mom coached her. Tiffeny loved the game from the start. In no time she knew enough to be linesman for her mother's games. Tiffeny smiles. "The players would tip me for doing it. I made pretty good money."

Her father lives in nearby Portland, but they've never met. She knows little about him except that he was a good athlete in high school. Is she sad they've never met? Tiffeny tucks a strand of hair behind her ear and says quietly, "You know, it's one of those things in life, you can't miss what you never had."

Her journey to the national team was straightforward. She played club soccer and was invited to join the Olympic Development Program, where she was noticed by national team scouts. Sixteen years old and a high school senior, Tiffeny joined the U-20 National Team. Her first team trip to Bulgaria collided with her high school graduation, but she has no regrets. Going to Bulgaria was thrilling.

In 1990 she entered the University of Portland and played for the highly regarded soccer coach Clive Charles. Playing college soccer focused her. Clive Charles was a major reason why. Says Tiffeny, "He brings out a player's best. I definitely tried harder because of him." Hard enough to set records that included tying with Mia Hamm as the NCAA Division I all-time leading goal scorer, a record that was only recently broken.

In 1991 she was invited to attend a national team camp. For the next several years she played "on the bubble," a term used to describe players who only sometimes are selected to play with the team.

In 1994 Tiffeny made the qualifying team, which removed her from the bubble but presented new challenges. National team members are ranked according to number. Tiffeny explains, "I'd be sixteen or seventeen and fight my way up to fourteen or fifteen. Then I'd get there and the challenge would be to get more playing time."

Those early years never felt secure, not even after she scored three goals in the 1995 Women's World Cup. The 1996 Olympics proved to be the turning point. Tiffeny's performance was spectacular. Her winning goal against China in the final game captured the Gold Medal. Finally she felt like she belonged.

ON THE FIELD

Friends call her Tiff, but teammates call her Millie, mainly to distinguish her from the other Tiff on the team, Tiffany Roberts. Her love for tall iced double lattes is well known among teammates who weren't surprised at all when Tiffeny hopped off the team bus to buy one at a coffee bar she spotted. They'd just spent the day at Giants Stadium practicing for the 1998 Goodwill Games. Traffic through midtown Manhattan was almost at a standstill. It was hot. She was thirsty. "Let me out, bus driver!" she said to the man, who looked startled by her request. She touched his shoulder lightly. "Really, it's okay, I'll catch up to you." Twelve blocks later she hopped back on, barely breathing hard, with her favorite iced coffee clutched in her hand.

Tiffeny Milbrett has always played forward. The instinct to score developed young. She scored her first goal at age eight, a moment she remembers well. Early in the game she'd noticed the keeper was kicking short so little Tiffeny decided to camp outside the penalty box and wait. Sure enough, the keeper kicked another ball short. She grins. "Naturally, I pounced on it and scored."

Tiffeny Milbrett is a crowd pleaser, especially when she scores. On her route back to teammates, she's likely to do an Irish jig, a river dance, or even a somersault or two.

When she talks about soccer, words come quicker. Her hands move fast, as if sketching out the play on an invisible blackboard. "I love creating plays," she says, then explains exactly what she means.

She creates plays by making unpredictable runs into space with the ball, by initiating combination passes, by dragging defenders with runs that create space for teammates, and by finishing when the scoring chance is there. Creating danger for defenders marking her is a challenge she loves. Says Tiffeny, "I can take defenders on, or go by them. I try to set up defenders by not making the same run or passing pattern twice, which is the ultimate fun of this game for me."

Her first appearance with the WNT was in 1991. Since then Tiffeny Milbrett has scored forty-seven goals and made thirty-two assists. Fellow striker Mia Hamm is so often involved in her moments near the goal that game announcers refer to them as the deadly duo.

In the mid-1990s Tiffeny played soccer in Japan for three consecutive seasons. Though not an easy transition, Tiffeny wanted to play during WNT's downtime. Japan offered the opportunity, so for six months each year she lived there.

Her intensity for the game has, at times, caused problems. She explains, "If I see a chance to score and the ball doesn't come at me, I get frustrated. Sometimes I say things I shouldn't, which isn't good." More than a few times her temper has caused trouble with the refs. "I'm working on that because at this level you can only focus on what you do. Focusing outside yourself only wastes energy."

Best game moment: Tiffeny scored the winning goal in the final game against China in the 1996 Olympics. Surely that had to be her best moment, right? She shakes her head. "Actually, my best game moment happened in my senior year of college when we beat Stanford in the NCAA quarter-finals, because that win put us in the Final Four." The University of Portland women's soccer team had never made the NCAA Final Four before. Tiffeny scored both goals of the game, but that's not why the memory brings tears to her eyes. "It's because of what it meant. We'd always been the underdogs. Finally we were contenders." Adding to the sweetness was the fact that the NCAA Final Four was held at the University of Portland. Tiffeny Milbrett played her last soccer game for the Pilots on home soil.

Red card: In a game played in Japan, Tiffeny was ejected after receiving two yellow cards. Both came from slide tackling. "I was trying to deflect a pass. The ref thought I was dangerous," she says as a small smile spreads across her face. "They're ticky-tacky about those things over there!"

Superstitions/lucky clothing/rituals: Four hours before game time, Tiffeny eats mild-tasting foods like chicken breast and pasta without spicy sauce. Otherwise, her only daily ritual is a visit to Starbucks. "It's a must," she says.

In the zone: "I don't hear anything when I'm in the zone," says Tiffeny. "The crowd, my teammates, nothing. During the final game of the Olympics, I didn't hear a thing the entire time I was on the field. Only when I got subbed out did I hear the 76,000 screaming fans. It's an intense feeling that I don't get that often."

Injuries: A bad sprain in her left ankle in 1997 kept her from playing for one month. Since then Tiffeny has had both ankles wrapped before games and practices.

Jersey number: In high school and college her favorite number was 15. When she joined WNT, 15 was taken, so Tiffeny took the number 16.

Blooper: In a high school game her team was losing 8–0. "Something snapped" when the other team scored their ninth goal. Says Tiffeny, "I just couldn't take it anymore. That ninth goal did me in. When we moved back for kickoff, I just sat down and folded my arms like a four-year-old in the middle of a temper tantrum. Awful to admit, but it happened!"

SOCCER IS MY LIFE

Tiffeny didn't decide to make soccer her career until college. Before then, she kept her options open. One thing was certain: she would be successful. That desire burned early. Her mother set the example by showing Tiffeny what it takes: hard work and heart. Once Tiffeny decided on soccer, it was a matter of applying those principles.

With Clive Charles as her coach, concentrating on soccer in college came easy. Sounding almost wistful, Tiffeny says of those years, "It was the essence of what playing soccer is about. We felt such camaraderie then. We were so young, so full of ourselves. It was such a wonderful time."

Commitment to her career may keep her

from meeting Mr. Right. Says Tiffeny, "I don't have time for anything that takes my energy because the game takes it all. He'd have to be an awfully special person to understand that. I haven't found him yet."

Putting herself first is a message Elsie Milbrett-Parham reinforced during her daughter's young years. She knew Tiffeny had talent. She also knew young girls often put aside their talents when boys entered the picture. Tiffeny laughs as she recalls her dating years in high school. "I'd bring a guy home, and Mom would say, 'He's very nice, Tiff; why don't you keep him as a friend?'"

ON INSPIRATION

Early on, her mom's example inspired Tiffeny to reach for the stars. Says Tiffeny, "Mom always said, 'With heart, you'll find a way.'" Support received from youth soccer coaches and their families inspired Tiffeny to excel. "I've been blessed. All my coaches took such good care of a precious little spirit that could have easily been broken with one tainted word."

Great coaching made her choose the University of Portland over schools that had better winning records. She wanted to become a quality player. She believed Coach Clive Charles could help her. Says Tiffeny, "Once I started playing for him, soccer took on a whole new perspective. I wanted to give it everything I had. I thank Clive for that. He's a mentor to many people because he's such a good man. Ask anyone who knows him. We all say the same thing. He's inspirational."

ADVICE TO YOUNG ATHLETES

Tiffeny doesn't direct her advice to gifted athletes who come from modest means, simply because those kids already know that in order to get to the next level, they must have heart. Says Tiffeny, "I wonder about the gifted athletes who have everything given to them. How do they find the hunger?" To those young athletes, Tiffeny frames her advice into a question. "Do you have the heart to push yourself? If you don't, find a way to get it because talent will only get you so far. You've got to be hungry. You've got to have heart. That's just reality."

Tiffeny Milbrett encourages young athletes to play several sports before focusing on one. "I get annoyed with coaches who tell young kids to play only one sport. Exposure benefits kids, especially those who have the goods, the talent, to go all the way. When time comes to choose one, they can say, 'I want to do this because I like playing it best.'"

FACTS

Caps: 102

Goals: 47

Assists: 32

Sponsor: Nike.

Causes: Boys & Girls Club of America.

Coaching/camps: Soccer clinics' coach.

Awards (partial list): 4-time All-American; 1990 Soccer America Magazine's Player of the Year; 4-time University of Portland MVP; 3-time West Coast Conference Player of the Year; 1995 FIFA Women's World Cup Bronze Medal; 1996 Olympic Games Gold Medal.

FAVORITES

Foods: Yakiniku, Japanese barbecue meat; iced tall double latte; Thai and Indian.

The U.S. Women's National Soccer Team

Hobbies: Hanging out at coffee bars with friends, making mixes of favorite music for friends, cooking.

Movies: *Back to the Future, Fried Green Tomatoes, Out of Africa, Somewhere in Time.*

Movie stars: Tom Cruise, Gillian Anderson, Jennifer Aniston.

TV shows: *The X-Files, Friends, Party of Five, Frasier, Just Shoot Me,* soccer games.

★ ★ ★

Carla Overbeck

PERSONAL STATS

Position: Central defender
Height: 5'7"
Weight: 128
Birthday: 5/9/68

SOCCER TEAMS

1973–1976 Blue Sharks, Spring Valley
Athletic Association
1977–1979 Killer Sharks
1979–1986 The Sting, The Sting Soccer Club
1994–present The Raleigh Wings Club
1987–present U.S. WNT

Prior to the 1996 Olympics, the usually reserved Carla Overbeck, wearing a leopard leotard, posed for a photo in Newsweek *magazine. She looked fabulous. Teammates took one look at their captain and immediately started calling her "Sheena, Queen of the Jungle."*

IN THE BEGINNING

"Dad called me Termite. I wasn't very big," says Carla Overbeck. When she speaks, a hint of Texas remains in her voice. She was raised in Dallas, a city known for its love for both American football and the other *futbol,* soccer.

At five Carla joined her first team. Smitten instantly, she slept in her uniform the night before each game. Says Carla, "Mom would say, 'Carla, you'll look a mess by game time,' but I didn't care. I wanted to be dressed. I wanted to be ready."

Loving the game wasn't the only reason she looked forward to playing. Sometimes soccer released her from yard duty. Her dad's pride and joy was the manicured lawn that looked like a putting green. Carla smiles, "Guess who kept it looking that way?"

She grew up in the Werden family with two older brothers and one older sister.

From babyhood, Carla was on soccer fields watching them play. All good athletes, they were also good at giving her grief. Says Carla, "I'm sure that's where my love for competition came from. I was always trying to beat them."

At age ten she finally earned some respect. One day she announced her intentions to enter a soccer juggling contest. Predictably, they teased her. A few days later she walked into the kitchen holding her first-prize ribbon. She smiles. "They were like, 'Wow Carla, you're okay.'"

She played on recreational teams for six years, then advanced to club soccer. Carla soon joined the Olympic Development Program's district team. Shifting allegiance was a tough adjustment. Carla explains, "The girls on my ODP team were the same girls I played against during regular season. It was weird getting used to that."

She liked ODP's intense focus on skills, though she didn't realize its role as a stepping-stone to the national team. That's why she didn't hesitate to say "no, thank you," when an invitation to an ODP regional summer camp conflicted with the Werden family's annual vacation to California.

In 1986 Carla entered the University of North Carolina at Chapel Hill. Though thrilled to be playing with the Tar Heels, her adjustment to college life was difficult. She was very homesick. For the first two years she cried often.

In the fall of her junior year, 1987, special circumstances brought her to the WNT. That summer Carla had made the Under-19 National Team. Her teammates, Mia Hamm, Julie Foudy, Joy Biefeld (Fawcett), and Kristine Lilly, were asked to join the WNT for a tournament in China. Carla wasn't. When the team arrived in China, WNT captain April Heinrichs received sad news. Her father had died. The coaching staff tracked Carla down in California to ask her to join them. Carla says, "I figured I'd be with them for one tournament."

ON THE FIELD

Listening to her talk about soccer, it's easy to understand why Carla Overbeck spends WNT off-hours coaching the women's varsity team at Duke University. She's a natural teacher. Her communication style is simple and direct: people unfamiliar with the game understand. Players in need of instruction learn.

Until 1995 Carla played sweeper, a defender

who always provides cover. After the 1995 World Cup the coaching staff changed systems. The team's poor cup showing, third place, was the reason. Though Carla agreed with the change in theory, putting it into practice took time. Carla liked playing sweeper. She explains, "In the system we used to play, a sweeper is free. You're always providing cover. If a player faces up to your defender, and tries to go around, that's where you are. You don't mark one man."

In the new system, called a zone defense system, her position changed to central defender. Though job responsibilities were similar in that she continued to organize and solve breakdowns, now Carla had to learn how to mark one man. In this system, the field is divided into zones, with one defender covering each zone. When opposing players enter, that defender marks man to man. Carla snaps her fingers and says, "It's not my nature to step up and down a player immediately, so it took me a while to adjust."

Her experience at UNC helped hone her leadership style. By 1991 the National Team coaching staff took notice and put her in charge any time captain April Heinrichs wasn't on the field.

What characteristic makes her a good

leader? Carla laughs, "I'm bossy. Actually, it's just my personality. I'm supportive on the field but also not afraid to let someone know she's doing something she shouldn't be doing."

Carla sees her role as a link between the coaching staff and players. When issues arise that aren't understood by one side or the other, she acts as a translator or facilitator. Carla says, "One of the joys of this team, the whole staff, in fact, is that communication is open. We say what's on our minds. Generally, there's no need to intercede."

When asked about the WNT's remarkable win/loss record, Carla Overbeck responds like a coach. Knocking on wood, she says, "People's expectations sometimes scare me. On any given day China, Norway, Denmark, or Germany could win. We never assume. One mistake could cost us a game."

The expression, "You've come a long way, baby" could be the Women's National Team anthem. Carla says, "Before 1991 winning the World Cup was our only goal. We didn't look beyond that. Winning was everything." After the win, things changed instantly. Carla snaps her fingers again. "Just like that, it changed. It took us a while to realize what it meant for women's soccer in this country."

Best game moment: Carla Overbeck's best game moment happened when the whistle blew in the final game against China in the 1996 Olympics. "We had worked so hard and there we were, gold medal winners."

Red card: None.

Superstitions/lucky clothing/rituals: She used to have a socks ritual. She wore them under shinguards. Also, the socks had to go on the same feet each time so she marked them L and R. Since changing shinguard brands, she doesn't need socks anymore.

In the zone: Carla doesn't experience "the zone."

Injuries: She knocks on wood. "So far, nothing serious."

Jersey number: The number 4 was assigned to her when she joined the team.

Blooper: Her all-time blooper moment was witnessed by millions who watched WNT beat Sweden in the 1996 Olympic quarterfinal game. Carla explains, "We were up two to zero. They had a direct kick into the box. This Swedish player goes up and hits it. The ball deflects off my leg and goes into the upper *V*. I was not happy." Friends teased her. Carla smiles. One of my friends called me and said, "Hey Carla, I heard a sports announcer on TV say, 'And then it was Carla Overbeck . . . Oops!'"

SOCCER IS MY LIFE

In junior high school Carla ran track and played volleyball but did not play high school soccer. Still, everyone knew ODP soccer was number one, a fact that didn't please her track coach. When an important track meet conflicted with ODP, Carla chose ODP. The coach threatened to kick her off the team if she didn't show. Says Carla, "That's when I knew what soccer meant to me. I loved track, but it was okay that I couldn't run anymore."

Her pregnancy offered another reminder of the importance of the game. Though teammates had no doubt Carla would regain the conditioning lost during the pregnancy, Carla wasn't so sure. Says Carla, "In the last months of my pregnancy, I'd sit on the sidelines and watch new players come in and think, what if I can't get it back? What if I don't have the heart or the skills needed to make it back?"

No need to worry. She had plenty of both. Within two weeks of Jackson's birth, she was jogging. Seven weeks later Carla joined her team for a tournament in Germany. Says Carla, "I had to do it for myself. I had to know I could still play at that level, still play with my team."

Carla and Greg Overbeck raise their young son using the team approach. They live in Chapel Hill, North Carolina, where they met when Carla was a student at UNC. Greg co-owns three restaurants. His flexible work schedule means that when Carla isn't home being Mom, Greg is there being Dad. Carla believes their shared responsibility benefits Jackson. Says Carla, "He's a lucky boy. His daddy's great and he gets to be with him a lot."

When Mom goes on the road, Jackson almost always travels with her. When she can't tend to him, her mom or Joy Fawcett's mom are there acting as Grandma to the three WNT offspring. Teammates also chip in. Umbrella strollers and diaper bags are standard equipment. So are high chairs in the dining room. Sometimes Jackson sits next to his mom, sometimes he sits next to other WNT players, who all know his culinary likes and dislikes.

Following a tight schedule to make it all work is second nature to Carla Overbeck. What *isn't* is enjoying free time. Her husband is an avid golfer. Carla wants to like the game, but so far she's not so sure. Says Carla, "I can't see spending half a day walking behind a ball when there's so much else to do."

One morning she joined Greg on the greens even though she had a full day ahead, which included working out. With each stroke her anxiety mounted. On the third hole she hit a ball deep into the woods. A perfect opportunity lay waiting. Carla grabbed her bag, slung it over her shoulder, and began to jog. The clamor and clank of the clubs behind her made Greg's words hard to hear. "Where you going?" he yelled. "I'm just trying to get a little exercise," she yelled back. By the time he yelled, "You can't jog on a golf course!" Carla couldn't hear him. She hasn't golfed since.

Though her priorities have shifted to include a family, the WNT continues to rank high. She considers them family, too. "We've grown up together," says Carla. "When we're done with a tournament, we go home to our lives, but when we come back, in no time we jump right back in with each other. I know we'll be friends for life."

ON INSPIRATION

People closest to Carla Overbeck have always given her inspiration. Her sister and brothers top the list. Her parents inspired her, too. They divorced when she was in college, but their announcement wasn't a surprise. They had separated when Carla was in high school. Says Carla, "When I hear about divorce, immediately I think, 'Oh, those poor kids,' but it wasn't that way for us. My parents handled it so well. I really commend them for that."

She wants young soccer players to look up to the team because "We're not a bunch of jerks!" exclaims Carla. "We're good role models. That's why we try to be accessible. We want kids to know we're just like them. We all started out like them. We're no different at all."

Without intending to, Carla helped shatter certain stereotypes about women athletes when she had a baby and returned to the game. Says Carla, "Maybe women won't be so plagued by the fears I had. Maybe they won't be so filled with self-doubt. I had a baby, Joy Fawcett had two. We came back. They can, too."

Fans' admiration makes her want to play forever. Says Carla, "But we can't, that's why we feel such a great responsibility for promoting this game. When it comes time to pass the baton, we want to pass it to players who love this game the way we do."

ADVICE TO YOUNG ATHLETES

The recent introduction of big money into professional athletics prompts her to give this advice: "Look up to sports figures who deserve it."

Before the 1991 FIFA Women's World Cup, the WNT earned a meager wage, an unbelievable ten dollars a day. Many players worked part-time jobs to pay their bills. Others depended on families for support. Says Carla, "I remember when we finally got medical insurance. Now, that was a big deal! Most of us had graduated from college and weren't on our parents' policies anymore, so we played without medical coverage. Getting it was a coup."

Today, between salaries and endorsements, WNT players now make enough to live as professional athletes. Says Carla, "I'm glad we're finally making more, but making money is not why we play. If that was our goal, none of us would be here. Money has nothing to do with the passion you need to play this game."

Carla believes young athletes should play several sports. Focusing on one too early sets children up for burnout. For players serious about soccer, Carla says, "Take it to the highest level whether that's high school varsity, club, ODP, or the national team, and always try to play with players better than you. Otherwise, you'll never improve."

★　　★　　★

FACTS

Caps: 128

Goals: 7

Assists: 4

Sponsors: Fila.

Causes: Smoke-Free Kids, a soccer anti-smoking campaign.

Coaching/camps: Duke University, assistant coach, women's soccer team.

Awards (partial list): 3-time All American; 1986–89 4-time NCAA National Championship, UNC Tar Heels; 1991 FIFA World Cup winner; 1995 FIFA World Cup Bronze Medal; 1996 Olympic

Gold Medal; 1998 Goodwill Games Gold Medal.

FAVORITES

Foods: Chocolate; any food served at Squid's, 411 West, or 518 West, her husband's three restaurants in Chapel Hill and Raleigh.

Hobbies: Reading.

Movies: *The Shawshank Redemption.*

Movie stars: Harrison Ford, Denzel Washington, Meg Ryan, Tom Hanks

TV shows: *The Rosie O'Donnell Show, The Oprah Winfrey Show.*

★ ★ ★

Cindy Parlow

PERSONAL STATS

Position: Forward
Height: 5'11"
Weight: 145
Birthday: 5/8/78

SOCCER TEAMS

1983–85 St. Paul's Team

1985–86 GASA Turtles

1986–91 Fury

1991–95 Memphis Futbol Club

1992–95 Germantown H.S. Varsity Team

1993–94 U-16 National Team

1994–95 U-21 National Team
1995–present U.S. WNT

*C*indy Parlow noshes on sour Gummi Bears
  *as she tells the story about the autographed
poster of the 1991 Women's World Cup champions hanging on her bedroom wall. Weeks after
the cup win, then thirteen-year-old Cindy
attended an ODP camp. Several WNT players
dropped by. Carla Overbeck was one.*

*Cindy pops another Gummi Bear into her
mouth and recalls the moment she tried to ask
Carla for her autograph. "When I got so close, I
was like, 'Oh, my gosh, there's Carla Overbeck!'
I mean, I couldn't believe . . ."*

*Suddenly Cindy stops speaking. Her face
prunes up, eyes tear. She pats her chest, reaches
for water, takes a gulp, and says softly, "Eh,
excuse me, but I'm having a little sour moment
here."*

*When it passes, she finishes the story. "I
chickened out so my mom got the poster
signed."*

IN THE BEGINNING

Cindy Parlow is tall and willowy with long
honey-colored blond hair and a creamy com-

plexion that blushes pink when given reason. Her accent is lightly southern. Soft. Genteel. At first meeting, she seems bashful, a kind of shyness that instantly evaporates when certain subjects are mentioned. Like boyfriends. Grabbing the tape recorder, she blares, "Attention! This is off the record!" then laughs loudly, revealing another side of the 1996 Olympic National Team's youngest player, a young woman who likes to goof around.

One of four children, Cindy has two older brothers and one younger. Everyone played soccer. They grew up in Memphis, Tennessee, not exactly a hotbed for soccer, according to Cindy. Remembering her first soccer team triggers bad memories. Why? Her head shakes slowly in disgust and she says, "We had green jerseys so the team voted on the name Turtles. Can you believe it?" Why didn't she like the name? Says Cindy, "Turtles are slow! Turtles hide in their shells! Turtles are scared! Why would any soccer player like that name?"

Because girls teams were scarce, Cindy played on several boys teams. She didn't mind. Playing with boys gave her an edge. Says Cindy, "Generally, they're gonna be faster and stronger, so they bring your game up. When you switch to girls teams, you're really prepared." The experience was beneficial, but not always easy. Some boys didn't want her to play. Or worse, they'd let her play but insist on treating her differently. How did she handle it? "I'd try to foul the heck out of them just to show them I wasn't afraid of contact. My attitude was, win the ball if you can, but next time I'm gonna try to keep you from getting it, and one of these times, I'm gonna beat you."

Throughout grammar school and high school, Cindy excelled in academics and played soccer, basketball, and softball. Admittedly, the schedule filled her days. Often, homework got done in the car while driving from one practice to another.

At thirteen she made the Olympic Development Program, where she learned enough about the soccer hierarchy to know that first, she wanted to play soccer for the University of North Carolina at Chapel Hill, then for the Women's National Team.

At fourteen she joined the U-16 Junior National Camp. In the fall of 1995 Cindy entered the University of North Carolina. The following winter, she was invited to join the Olympic Games training camp. Weeks later the roster for the 1996 Olympic Team was posted. Cindy Parlow's name was on it. She called home expecting her parents to be ecstatic. When they heard the news, the Parlows congratulated their daughter and said, "We've got to go." Their reaction surprised her. "What's the hurry?" she wanted to know. Cindy smiles. "My mother says to me, 'Well, honey, this *is* the Olympics, after all. Hotels book up quick. We've got to make our reservations.'"

ON THE FIELD

Her head turbaned in a towel, another wrapped around her body, Cindy Parlow walks past several WNT players sitting in the shower room. Someone whistles. Someone else says, "Now, don't you look cute!" Their teasing eggs her on. She starts to sashay, a lopsided verson of what a beauty pageant contestant might look like promenading down a runway.

When seventeen-year-old Cindy Parlow joined the team, they took her under wing immediately. Her first roommate-on-the-road was Brandi Chastain, the perfect combination of old and new. Says Cindy, "Brandi had just returned to the team, so in a way, she was new, too, plus she had all this experience with them which was just so helpful."

In her first WNT game, Cindy scored two

goals against Brazil that won it for her team.
The Brazilian press, world-renowned for both
their love of soccer and suspicion of women
playing it, couldn't resist. The teenage forward
made all the Brazilian newspapers. Says
Cindy, "It was a great way to start out with the
team."

Her college career started off with a bang,
too. At the end of her first season Cindy
Parlow was ranked the number one scorer of
the UNC Tar Heels, inviting comparisons with
UNC alum Mia Hamm.

Juggling college and the WNT can be tricky.
During the fall season, Cindy plays with her
college team. In the spring she travels with
WNT as much as her academic schedule per-
mits. Says Cindy, "If we have several tournaments out of the country, I may only be able to
make one, so Tony [DiCicco] decides where I'd
best be utilized and that's where I go."

She is a fierce competitor who always puts
her team's needs first. When asked about new
players joining the team, Cindy says, "Our
goals are to win gold medals and world championships. In order to do that, we want the
best personnel there is. Obviously, I want to be
one, but more important, I want my team to
win. If my playing means we can't do that,

then take me off the field. This isn't about me. It's about my team."

Best game moment: When Cindy made the WNT roster in 1996, she was already a star player on the Junior National Team. Her best moment came during a championship game when she scored the winning goal. Says Cindy, "On that team I was one of the players they depended on to bring them to the next level, so when I scored that goal, it was just awesome."

Red card: "No!" answers Cindy Parlow. She's never been ejected from the game. Really? She grimaces. "Do we have to go there?" With nudging, she does, but first delivers this disclaimer: "Remember, this happened when I was very young and very stupid."

Her ODP state team was up against a team known to be dirty players. Says Cindy, "This girl keeps hacking away at me, even when I didn't have the ball. This one time she came at me hard, and I don't know, something just snapped inside and I punched her," she says quietly. Punched her? A pained look covers her face. "Yep. It was a stupid thing to do. I didn't even wait until the ref wasn't looking. Shoot, I was totally young, I know that's no excuse, but that's what happened."

Superstitions/lucky clothing/rituals: She eats lightly before games. Pasta or a baked potato are favorites.

In the zone: She played in the zone once, during a championship high school basketball game. Her team was the underdog. Cindy was on fire. The game went into overtime. With her team down by one, she drew a foul and went to the free-throw line. Her two baskets won the game. Afterward, a local reporter asked how she felt about making fifteen of sixteen baskets. Cindy couldn't answer. She says, "I had no idea I scored thirty points." Nor did she hear the roar of the crowd throughout the game, or the announcer's drone, "Parlow again" each time she put one in. Says Cindy, "I haven't felt that yet in soccer, but I hope to."

Injuries: A torn MCL in high school. The injury is a common malady of soccer players.

Jersey number: She wore number 3 during the Olympics, then switched to number 12 after Carin Gabarra retired. "I just didn't think three was a forward's number. Don't ask me why, I just didn't."

Blooper: Her high school soccer team had earned a reputation as one of the best in the state. The University of Arkansas challenged them to a game. College coaches were there. Cindy's team was down 1–0. In the last few minutes she got the ball. Says Cindy, "I had a clear shot. I'm running, no one was catching me. I get to the top of the box and take my shot." A sure goal that never made it in. Somehow the cleat on one shoe tangled up into the lace on the other, and Cindy went down hard. Spectators began to laugh. Did she? "What else could I do?" Did they win? She mumbles, "That's not important."

SOCCER IS MY LIFE

Cindy Parlow gave up high school memories for the chance to play on the U.S. Women's National Team. That's how much she loves the game. The year was 1995. Cindy was a junior in high school. It was springtime in Memphis and dinnertime at the Parlow house. Usually, she didn't talk much at the table. With three brothers, those who talked most ate least. But that night she made an exception. Cindy had it all figured out. In order to make the Olympic Team roster, she needed to train at the very highest level. She remembers saying, "Eh, Mom, Dad, I'd like to go to UNC." The Parlows already knew Cindy dreamed of playing soccer there, so they didn't treat the announcement as news. Then Cindy said, "I want to go next fall." That was news. Cindy was sixteen. The following fall was supposed to be her senior year in high school, not freshman year in college. But Cindy knew if she had any prayer of making the WNT, she needed the edge that playing at UNC would give her.

Her mom wasn't crazy about her daughter's leaving home a year early, so she told Cindy that if she wanted this, she'd have to make it happen. Cindy did. After jumping over several hurdles that included taking correspondence school courses and getting NCA waivers signed, the following fall semester Cindy Parlow entered UNC. Her high school senior class would have to carry on without her.

Her dream to play with WNT began years earlier. Making the Junior National Team made it more real. She remembers the first time she saw the WNT play up close. She was at a Junior National training camp. Her team sat on benches snapping photos of the national team practicing in front of them. Says Cindy, "We couldn't believe we were on the same field with them." It got better. A few days later she was invited to scrimmage with the WNT. She smiles. "I was so nervous, I was like, 'Oh my gosh, I'm playing with the national team.'"

Nerves didn't get the better of her. She played well enough to be invited back by the WNT's coach, Anson Dorrance. He told her to attend a team meeting. There, he asked Julie Foudy and Kristine Lilly to teach Cindy how to play in the midfield.

That afternoon Cindy paid them a visit in their hotel room and watched them finish playing a board game. Cindy says, "I remember standing there looking at them play and saying to myself over and over, 'Oh my gosh, oh my gosh.'"

ON INSPIRATION

When Michelle Akers received her one and only red card, Cindy Parlow was in the stadium watching. She was thirteen years old at the time. Says Cindy, "It was a lousy call.

When she got thrown out, I was like, 'Way to go, Michelle.'"

For many reasons Michelle Akers has been inspirational. Some are obvious: like Cindy, Michelle is tall. Also like Cindy, she's played both forward and in the midfield. Other reasons are obvious only to fans, like Cindy Parlow, who have followed this team since its formation in 1985. Cindy says, "Back then, the team didn't draw many fans, at least not like today, but that didn't matter to Michelle. She was the one quoted in newpapers, the one doing the interviews on the field, always talking up the game whenever she had the chance. We owe her a lot."

ADVICE TO YOUNG ATHLETES

Her advice about soccer is simple. "Soccer is a game. It will always be just a game, so make sure you're having fun." Her advice, in general, reflects her interests. Cindy Parlow is a nutrition major who someday hopes to work as a registered dietitian. The culture's preoccupation with skinniness concerns her. Says Cindy, "If you look at all of us on the team, we're fit, no one is overweight, but none of us is skinny. Kids need to understand that eating a certain amount of fat is not only okay, it's necessary to maintain proper functioning of the body."

Does she see a shift away from the rail-thin model image now that women are into athletics? Yes and no. Says Cindy, "I think we are shifting the image, but we've got a ways to go. I learned something recently that really surprised me. Something like thirty percent of all female college students have eating disorders. Of that group, about thirty-five percent are athletes. What we all have to do is learn how to stand up to that pressure and say, 'No thanks. Emaciated isn't pretty. That's not how I want to look.'"

FACTS

Caps: 42

Goals: 17

Assists: 3

Sponsors: College students cannot have sponsors, according to NCAA rules.

Coaching/camps: UNC soccer camps; Gold Medal Soccer Camp.

FAVORITES

Food: Steak and mashed potatoes.

Hobbies: Reading, in-line skating.

Movies: *Hunt for Red October; Patriot Games; The Fugitive; Top Gun; Lethal Weapon 1, 2, 3, and 4.*

Movie stars: Harrison Ford.

TV shows: *ER.*

* * *

Tiffany Roberts

PERSONAL STATS

Position: Midfield defender
Height: 5'3"
Weight: 113
Birthday: 5/5/77

SOCCER TEAMS

1983–1984 Canaries, San Ramon Soccer Club
1985–1986 Snowbirds, San Ramon Soccer Club
1987–1993 Lightning, Alcosta Soccer Club
1987–1993 Tri Valley Stars, Premier League
1995–1998 University of North Carolina Tar
Heels
1993–present U.S. WNT

*S*he's young. She's hip. She wears a nose ring, *blasts hip-hop to pump up before games, chews gum on the field, and has even engaged in a fistfight or two. Explains the dark-haired, petite WNT defender, "But that was in my younger days. I'm much more mellow now!"*

IN THE BEGINNING

Tiffany Roberts's dream of winning gold medals began early. Proof hangs on the family-room wall in her parents' home in San Ramon, California. A crayon drawing sketched by second-grader Tiffany depicts a little girl standing on the Olympic podium. Three gold medals dangle from her neck: one for soccer, one for gymnastics, and one for track. Tiffany says, "I guess I didn't know women weren't competing in soccer back then."

The baby and only daughter of Dave and Rose Roberts's family of four, Tiffany played her first soccer game at age five. That game earned her her first community newspaper headline: "Tiny Tiffany Roberts Scores Six Goals."

Her dad's own athletic ability made him recognize a steeliness in Tiffany most kids didn't possess. Although his only daughter was always the tiniest on the field, she was also the most aggressive. "Dad used to call me his determined little player," says Tiffany of the man she calls Mr. Mom. Both parents worked, but her dad's job close to home made him the family chauffeur. When he dropped her off at practice, he always stayed to watch.

Coaches also took notice that tiny Tiffany loved to slide-tackle players twice her size. Where does her fearlessness come from? "Try being the youngest and the only girl with three older brothers," explains Tiff. "You learn real quick how to fight back."

It was that determination that inspired WNT head coach Tony DiCicco to nickname her Little Animal. DiCicco's predecessor, Anson Dorrance, saw it, too. During one pregame pep talk, to illustrate how he wanted his players to cover space, Dorrance drew a big heart covering a soccer field and said, "Take it from Tiff." Tiffany explains her drive this way. "I don't know where it comes from, I only know I like to win, always have, so maybe that's it."

With Tiffany Roberts on the roster, her community soccer teams rarely lost. Her older brother John coached her first team. Instantly she fell in love with the game, even though it competed with her two other loves, gymnastics and track. When the time came to choose one sport, was it a tough decision? Tiffany answers, "Not really. By then I knew that what I loved about soccer was playing on a team."

Growing up, Tiffany always played forward. For one season when she was little, Tiffany played with WNT teammate Kate Sobrero. Tiffany says, "I think we were nine. The coach's only strategy all season long was get the ball to me or Kate. We were his little scoring machines." Soccer got serious when Tiffany began playing for a club team called Lightning, the team that taught her how to be a team player. "We were like a family," says Tiffany of the six years she played with them. At age fourteen her coach told Tiffany to try out for the Olympic Development Program's California state team. Not only did she make the cut, Tiffany became its youngest player.

From the start, ODP coaches had confidence in her ability, more than she had in herself. She says, "I didn't know what they saw in me. The other girls were older and more experienced, so naturally, I looked up to them." A tournament in Oregon gave her a confidence boost. "The coaches' strategy was 'When you get the ball, find Tiff'—I knew they wouldn't be saying that if they didn't think I could get the job done."

At sixteen she joined the WNT and juggled school work and soccer with the help of supportive high school teachers. In three and a half years she graduated from high school. The following fall Tiffany entered the University of North Carolina at Chapel Hill. Between school, college soccer, and WNT, does she have time for fun? She offers a wry smile. "Oh, I manage."

ON THE FIELD

"They call me Tiff, T.R., Saucy, Pino, or Little Animal, take your pick," says the young woman known for her superior physical endurance and unyielding determination. At her first WNT international game, Tiffany Roberts received a yellow card. She smiles, "Actually, it was within the first thirty seconds of the game. I think I set a record."

Her diminutive size has always caused opponents to underestimate her impact on the field, which is just fine with Tiffany Roberts. She plays midfield defender, a position reserved for players in top physical form because it requires constant motion. Midfielders either defend against penetration or lead the assault to score. Running for the ninety minutes is not a problem for Tiffany Roberts, which is why some press members have nicknamed her Energizer Bunny. From start to finish, Tiffany Roberts keeps running. Literally. Her ability to sustain a heart rate of over two hundred beats per minute for an entire game without collapsing has made her the subject of several research studies.

Best game moment: "Definitely the semifinal game in the ninety-six Olympics," says Tiffany. "I loved the final game, but as a player, my best contribution came during the semifinal." They played Norway, the 1995 World Cup winners. Mia Hamm sat out because of injury. Tony DiCicco gave Tiffany one job to do: guard the player then considered the best woman soccer player in the world, Hege Rise. Tiffany says, "Tony told me, 'You gotta stay in her shorts all game,' which meant I couldn't let her assist or score." Tiffany did the job. "That was a big game for me."

Red card: Tiffany was a junior in high school when she received her first and only red card. The game was against her school's arch rival.

Tiffany says, "I was convinced they were out to get me. I kept getting pummeled every time I got the ball. This one time I got the ball and totally shanked it. I was on the ground getting up when this player came over and pushed me back down. 'What's your problem?' I yelled. Next thing I knew, her teammates piled on top and just started beating on me. I got a few swings in before the refs broke it up. I got red-carded and so did the player who started the fight. I was so mad."

Superstitions/lucky clothing/rituals: Tiffany puts a fresh piece of gum in her mouth before each game. Does she chew during the game? Yes, she does. Her lucky piece of jewelry is her nose earring. How does she get away with wearing it during games? A hint of mischief washes across her face. "Refs may think I wear it for religious reasons." Where do they get that notion? Tiffany isn't saying.

In the zone: When Tiffany Roberts plays in the zone, she feels total confidence. She explains, "I was definitely in the zone during the Olympics. I played the best soccer I've ever played then. It was a great feeling." What's it feel like? "I feel like I can do anything. I'm having a blast! That's what it feels like."

Injuries: Torn knee cartilage required surgery after the 1996 Olympics. Because she resumed playing too soon, she reinjured the knee and had to have a second surgery. This time, to insure a complete recovery, she skipped spring season with the WNT. By the following fall she was back on the field.

Jersey number: Says Tiffany, "I've worn number five forever. My birthday is five/five. I love fives."

Blooper: Tiffany's creamy complexion flushes pink when she recalls the day she made 10,000 fans laugh. They were playing Brazil in a Texas stadium packed with fans. Tiffany was playing back. Carla Overbeck sent her a ball. All alone with no one yelling, "Man on! Man on!" Tiffany began to dribble the ball down the field when *splat!* she tripped over her own feet and landed hard on the ground. The initial gasp of the crowd turned into a group laugh rippling through the stadium. At this point in the story Tiffany covers her face with her French-manicured hands. Finally she peeks out. "You can bet I didn't want to get up. My teammates yelling 'Sniper! Sniper!' didn't make it any easier!"

SOCCER IS MY LIFE

The Women's National Team formed when Tiffany Roberts was eight years old. Two years later, in 1987, she set this goal: work hard enough to join the WNT. Five years later she did. The year was 1993. Tiffany was just sixteen. By then she had advanced to the regional ODP team. They played in a Thanksgiving tournament in Boca Raton, Florida, where National Team's U-16 and U-20 team coaches spotted her. Could she stay another week? they asked. In Tiffany's mind, she was being considered for the U-20 National Team. That week at the training camp the U-20 coach, Clive Charles, approached her on the field. "We're going to drive you down to Fort Lauderdale, where the women are playing," Charles explained. Tiffany's reaction was typical of a sixteen-year-old. "I thought he was joking so I said 'You've made a mistake.'" What happened next made her a believer. "He walked me over to Anson Dorrance [then WNT's head coach] and said, 'T.R. wants to make sure she heard me right.' Dorrance smiled at me and said, 'you heard right, you're with the big girls now.'" Her first reaction? Tiffany smiles, "I called my dad. He was so tickled."

She was a starter from the beginning. Tiffany thinks she knows why. At her first training camp, WNT scrimmaged a U-16 boys team at Stanford University. She didn't score but her performance made an impression, especially the header she went up for against an opponent twice her size. From that day on, coaches called her fearless. Says Tiffany, "I'm not the most technical or skillful player on this team. My value to this team is my mental attitude. I just don't like to get beat."

ON INSPIRATION

Track star Jackie Joyner-Kersee and gymnast Mary Lou Retton are athletes Tiffany admires, but when it comes to inspiration, her dad tops the list. Tiffany smiles. "He's always there for me. He's my number one fan. When I was little, he'd always stay at practice shagging balls or doing whatever the coach needed him to do. He's an incredible guy."

Tiffany likes being an inspiration to young players, especially Asian players. Her mom is

Filipino. The community has embraced its Olympic Gold Medalist. Tiffany says, "The first story ever written about me was in a prominent Filipino magazine, *Filipinas*. I get a kick out of talking to Asian kids—all kids for that matter—about the game. Talking to groups is fun, and for some reason, I'm not shy at all!"

ADVICE TO YOUNG ATHLETES

Tiffany's mom always says, "If you want it bad enough, you'll find a way to get it." Good advice that Tiffany passes on. She also cautions young players to stay focused on the whole picture. Tiffany explains, "It's not easy to succeed at school and at soccer. It's a challenge to make everything work." In high school she had no problem. College was another story. Tiffany winces as she recalls her freshman year at the University of North Carolina. "I was playing good soccer and I was having a really good time. However, I wasn't studying." An embarrassing first semester grade point average provided the incentive needed to get back on track and back on the dean's list. With a major in communications, she hopes someday to become a broadcast journalist, but that will have to wait until she retires from the game.

★　★　★

FACTS

Caps: 67

Goals: 6

Assists: 5

Sponsor: College students cannot have sponsors, according to NCAA rules.

Causes: Outreach to young athletes through community organizations.

Coaching/camps: UNC soccer camps, 1997, 1998.

Awards (partial list): 1994 Umbro National Player of the Year; 3-time Parade All American; 1995 Parade Player of the Year; 1995 California State Player of the Year; 1994 Tiffany Roberts Day in San Ramon, California; 1996 and 1997 NCAA Champions, University of North Carolina; 1995 FIFA Women's World Cup Bronze Medal; 1996 Olympic Games Gold Medal.

FAVORITES

Foods: Macaroni and cheese, prime rib, Filipino food, mashed potatoes.

Hobbies: Shopping; sunbathing; listening to music—R&B, hip-hop, rap; dancing.

Movies: *Sixteen Candles, Clueless, Happy Gilmore, Grease.*

Movie stars: Meg Ryan, Claire Danes, Leonardo DiCaprio, Adam Sandler, John Travolta.

TV shows: *Friends, The Oprah Winfrey Show,* MTV.

★ ★ ★

Briana Scurry

PERSONAL STATS

Position: Goalkeeper
Height: 5'8"
Weight: 140
Birthday: 9/7/71

SOCCER TEAMS

1984–1990 Brooklyn Park Kickers
1990–1993 University of
    Massachusetts–Amherst
1993–present U.S. WNT

*T*he press sometimes describes Briana Scurry
as angry or intense-looking. Says Briana,
*"That's my game face. I'm like a light switch.
When I walk off the field, I'm a completely different person."*

*You believe her. She smiles and her face lights
up with mischief, revealing the other Briana
Scurry: the one who came home from Mardi
Gras with a panther tattooed on her left shoulder, the one who ran naked down a Georgia
street the night they won the gold medal. The
other Briana Scurry is a bit of a daredevil.*

IN THE BEGINNING

Briana Scurry dreamed of winning a gold
medal at age eight. Back then, she didn't yet
play soccer, but she did run like the wind, so
she figured the medal would be in track. Says
Briana, "My friend Ted and I would run down
the streets throwing a broomstick like a
javelin, back and forth, back and forth, while I
announced the game, play by play." She turns
her fist into a microphone. "And it looks like
Briana Scurry breaks the world record and
wins the gold medal!"

She grew up in Dayton, Minnesota, a small
town outside the Twin Cities of St. Paul and

Minneapolis, the youngest in a blended family of nine children. Until fifth grade she played tackle football with boys in the under-75-pound division. Her career ended when time came to move up to the over-75-pound division. Says Briana, "Mom put her foot down. She was afraid I'd get hurt."

Her late start in soccer—she was almost twelve—is a consequence of her surroundings. Dayton had one field suitable for soccer. Only boys played, so once again Briana joined a boys team. The coach put her in goal to keep her from getting hurt. She did anyway, mostly because when players came at her, Briana Scurry would not back down.

The following year she joined a girls traveling team and switched positions. She wanted to play forward. Though she scored lots of goals, playing up front made her realize how much she missed playing in goal. Says Briana, "I loved the glory of scoring, but once the ball got past me, I'd get so nervous that I'd end up running back to help everybody out!"

At fourteen, Briana made the Olympic Development Program's state team. For the next two years she was invited to ODP regional camps but never made the regional team.

In high school Briana played varsity soccer, basketball, and track, and was named the best high school athlete in Minnesota. When time came to decide on colleges, her club coach led her to the University of Massachusetts. Why? Jim Rudy, the best goalkeeping coach in the country, was there. Says Briana, "I didn't have the advantage of ODP training, so I figured I was behind. With my athletic ability, I thought Jim could do something with me."

Jim Rudy already had a nationally known goalkeeper on his varsity team, so Briana didn't expect to play much. That was okay. She was there to learn. But he did play her in half the games, surprising everyone, including Briana. By senior year she had earned the All-American title and the attention of the Women's National Team.

ON THE FIELD

Goalkeepers say the thrill of playing in goal has to do with the feeling of control. Briana Scurry agrees. "When I'm keeper, I decide. If I can get anywhere near the ball, I can keep them from scoring. You don't have that feeling anywhere else."

Briana Scurry hates to lose. The bad taste

lingers. Four years after the 1995 World Cup, losing to Norway still puts a scowl on her face. The loss stunned the team. Briana says, "For the next year we were bombarded by this horrible, disgusting, nasty thing that happened to us. We couldn't get over it. We had too much pride to let Norway believe they were better." She shakes her head. "We knew we were better. That spurred us on all year long. We just couldn't get over it."

When feeling philosophical, she wonders if the '95 Cup loss was destined. Says Briana, "I swear we could have thrown the kitchen sink at them and it would have bounced off the crossbars! It just wasn't our time." But the feeling is fleeting when she remembers details of the game. Her scowl returns. "I have never been at a game that was so frustrating. I just hope we always remember what we felt like so we don't ever le that happen to us again."

Best game moment: Winning against Norway a year later proved that whatever virus had invaded the WNT no longer threatened their health. In sudden death at the semifinal match in the 1996 Olympics, Julie Foudy began a run that ended with Shannon MacMillan scoring the winning goal. Says Briana. "Once Shannon hit it, I knew it was going in 'cause I knew the goalkeeper couldn't get it." Her eyes travel off, as if watching the moment again. "When it went in, I took off in a dead sprint. I don't remember my feet touching the ground. That's when the tears came. That's when I cried for the first time. All that pent-up frustration finally let loose one year later."

Red card: She groans. "Yeah, I got one during the ninety-five Cup. We were playing Denmark and up two to nothing in the ninety-second minute. They shot a ball at me. It was easy, no problem. I punted it. Immediately, Denmark fans go nuts. No officials are near me. All of a sudden the linesman's flag goes up. The ref comes running at me and—*Bam!*—red-cards me. He assumed I handled the ball outside the box, which I didn't. I just looked at him and walked off the field. I did not blink, nor did I utter one word. The cameras were in my face waiting for me to blow, but I just stood there glaring."

Superstitions/lucky clothing/rituals: Before games, Briana grabs the crossbar and hangs. She also kneels on one knee and prays for a safe game.

In the zone: When Briana is in the zone, the ball looks really big. "It's like it has a rope attached to it. I move faster, make saves left and right. I don't know how to control it, but it's a great feeling when I'm in it."

Injuries: A car accident in 1995 left Briana with neck and back injuries that took time healing. She knocks on wood. "So far, I have no injuries from playing soccer."

Jersey number: Traditionally, a team's number one goalkeeper wears the number 1, Briana Scurry's number.

Blooper: Not quite a blooper, Briana wants to set the record straight about the night they won the gold medal and she ran naked down a Georgia street. As the story goes, one night a few months before the Olympic Games, *Sports Illustrated* called, collecting interesting facts about Olympic players. Says Briana, "They woke me up from a sound sleep and asked what I'd do if we won the gold. Half-awake, I said, 'I'll run naked through the streets of Georgia if we win' and hung up."

Days before the games commenced, the magazine printed the list that included

Briana's promise to run naked. Within seconds of winning, reporters wanted to know when she was going to make good on her promise. She knew she had to, but how? The answer came later that night at the victory celebration party. She and her roommate slipped away from the party at about two A.M. and drove to a small town outside Atlanta called Athens. With videocam in hand, her roommate recorded the moment. Wearing only her medal, Briana ran down a street and back, about twenty yards total. They returned to the party and showed the evidence to the president of Nike and one press person. *Sports Illustrated* wanted to see it—Briana said no. They persisted, promising if she let them print one photo, they'd only show her backside fuzzed out. Says Briana, "With my luck, they would have printed my front side and then my mother would have . . ." Her eyebrows arch up in disapproval. "I don't think so."

The tabloid papers got wind of her early morning run and inflated the event to scandal proportions by reporting that on a bet, Briana Scurry ran naked down a city block in Atlanta and everyone saw her. "It wasn't a bet. I said I was going to do it, and being a woman of my word, I did."

SOCCER IS MY LIFE

Briana Scurry wants to make one thing perfectly clear: soccer dominates her time, but it doesn't dominate her life. She concedes finding time for a personal life does present challenges, especially for a single player. Time away from home is the reason. During the season, players spend weeks traveling. Before big competitions like the World Cup and the Olympics, the WNT enters a residency camp for six months. Briana waves her hand pathetically and says, "You meet someone, it's going great, then it's bye-bye for the next six months!"

Though she was voted best high school goalkeeper in her state, Briana didn't think she ranked with the top-level players. Today, she traces her lack of confidence back to her experiences with ODP. Says Briana, "ODP left me believing I didn't compare with elite players, so that's why I didn't dream of making the national team." It wasn't until the summer before college when Briana was invited to play on the northwest regional team at the Olympic Sports Festival that she got a good look at the competition. Only then did she begin to dream about making the national team. Says Briana,

"I looked around and said to myself, I can do this. With proper coaching, I know I can."

Under the direction of University of Massachusetts coach Jim Rudy, her confidence soared. In her senior year the team made it to the NCAA Final Four. Unfortunately, their first game was against defending NCAA champions, the University of North Carolina's Tar Heels, the team coached by then-WNT coach Anson Dorrance and starring Mia Hamm and Kristine Lilly, to name a few. Says Briana, "They massacred us four to one. Mia scored off me in a penalty kick in the first eleven minutes."

In spite of the loss, she played a great game, making an unbelievable twenty-five saves. Afterward, the press asked for interviews. She had just finished talking to them and was walking through UNC's stadium when she spotted Mia Hamm walking toward her. Anson Dorrance was with her. Says Briana, "Mia passes me and says, 'Hey, Keeper, great game.' So I walked over, shook her hand, and whispered in her ear, 'Thanks, but tell him that, would ya?'" Briana smiles. "Mia whispered back, 'He already knows.'"

The next Monday, Briana was at school contemplating the future. When the season ended, so did her soccer-playing days. She had majored in political science with an eye on law. It was time to think about applying to law schools. A phone call changed those plans. Her coach called her into his office and told her not to hang up her cleats. The Women's National Team had called. She was going to camp.

Briana's reaction was immediate. "I was ecstatic. Here I was, an unknown, not in the ODP loop. My family had no clout. But I was going to the national team's training camp anyway."

Five days later she was playing with the Women's National Team. Says Briana, "So you see, you never know until you try."

ON INSPIRATION

"Parents who stand behind and not in front of their children will inspire them to succeed," says Briana Scurry. Though the Scurry's financial resources were limited, their faith in Briana wasn't. She says, "My parents were always there for me. When I set a goal, they believed I'd do it."

Growing up, Briana found inspiration from sports figures who physically looked like her. College basketball star Pearl Washington was one. "I even painted his number, thirty-one, on the heel of my cleats. That's how much I admired him." Basketball great Cheryl Miller also offered inspiration. "The WNBA owes her a world of debt for paving the way."

Being an inspiration to young people, especially African-American kids, pleases her. Says Briana, "You may have noticed, I'm the only African-American on this team. Soccer's not exactly big in urban areas." When asked why, she answers frankly. "Many African-Americans consider it an elitist, suburban sport"—a sport that needs grassy fields, a premium in urban areas where so many African-American kids live. Says Briana, "Lack of playing fields is a real problem."

She lives in Chicago and often speaks to inner-city kids about the game. Says Briana, "We need more African-Americans in this game. Besides me, there are very few, so it's important for me to help get the word out. Soccer's a great sport that offers great opportunities. Our kids need to know that."

ADVICE TO YOUNG ATHLETES

Briana's mom has always told her daughter "A girl's gotta do what a girl's gotta do." Says

Briana, "I tell kids, don't let any negative energy get you down. You may not get there by going through the front door. You may have to go through the back, but you can get there if you have desire. I know because that's how I did it."

Her admission onto the national team is a story she tells often even though it doesn't put the Olympic Development Program in the best light. Says Briana, "When I attended those two regional camps, I do believe they already had their teams picked out. I didn't know it back then, but ODP is a very political organization."

Though the rejection didn't stop her, the pain still lingers. "I remember the day they announced the players who'd made the regional pool. It was my second time at the camp and I believed I had a shot at it. Then they announced the goalkeeper. As the girl walked up, I remember thinking, 'Wow, how lucky can you be!'"

She smiles and repeats her mother's advice. "But all these years later here I am on the national team. 'A girl's gotta do what a girl's gotta do.'"

FACTS

Caps: 78

Sponsor: Nike.

Causes: AIDS awareness.

Coaching/camps: University of Massachusetts–Amherst, University of Arkansas.

Awards: 1989 top female athlete in Minnesota; 1993 consensus top goalkeeper; 1995 FIFA Women's World Cup Bronze Medal; 1996 Olympic Gold Medal; 1998 Goodwill Games Gold Medal.

FAVORITES

Foods: Lasagna, sushi.

Hobbies: Hiking, long walks

Movies: *Simon Birch, The Lion King.*

Movie stars: Julia Roberts.

TV shows: *Friends, South Park.*

★ ★ ★

Tisha Venturini

PERSONAL STATS

Position: Central midfielder
Height: 5'6"
Weight: 125
Birthday: 3/3/73

SOCCER TEAMS

1979–1982 The Koalas
1983–1985 Ajax Thunder (boys team)
1986–1992 Ajax Eclipse (girls team)
1987–1991 U-19 National Team
1991–present U.S. WNT

*T*he morning after the WNT beat Denmark in the quarterfinal round of the Goodwill Games, a fan approached Coach Tony DiCicco at the hotel and said, "Boy, you really work your players, don't you."

Coach DiCicco looked puzzled. "What do you mean?"

Said the fan, "Last night I almost ran into a couple of them running up and down the stairs after the game. Don't they even get time off for winning?"

The two players sprinting the seven-flight staircase were Tisha Venturini and Christie Pearce.

Coach DiCicco smiled. "I didn't tell them to do that. They do that all on their own."

IN THE BEGINNING

Tisha Venturini looks like the classic California girl, tall, tan, and lovely. High cheekbones accent big brown eyes. Her wide smile shows off straight white teeth. She speaks with a slight twang, partly from growing up in Modesto, a heartland region in California, partly from living in the South when she attended the University of North Carolina at Chapel Hill.

Tisha is the youngest of Dr. Alfred (Chick) and Lynda Venturini's three children. They all played soccer. Her older brother Todd introduced her to the game. He and friends used to play in their backyard, where little Tisha would hang out watching. One day the teams came up short a player. Tisha seized the moment. Todd's friends weren't sure they wanted to play with a girl until they saw what the four-year-old could do. From that day on, when it came time to choose sides, the five-and-a-half-year-old boys fought over who'd get Tisha.

When she was finally old enough to join her first community recreational team, five-year-old Tisha was already a seasoned player. Says Tisha, "I remember the coaches telling me, 'Tish, you can play whatever position you want.' I guess that's when I first knew that maybe I was pretty good."

She played several sports including tennis, softball, volleyball, and skiing, but soccer was the only one she played all the time. Each morning before school Tisha and the boys would play four-square on the street. They'd get so involved, that the bus driver often had to honk for their attention. Playing continued indoors, too. A long hallway in her home made the perfect indoor court. After trying in vain to stop her children from battering the walls with the ball, Tisha's mom finally surrendered and turned the hallway over to soccer.

Modesto, California, was not a big soccer community. By age ten, Tisha needed the kind of challenge girls recreational teams could not provide. One afternoon a coach from an under-twelve boys traveling team called Tisha's dad. He'd heard about the girl with the blond braids. Did she want to try out for his team? Thinking his daughter didn't want that kind of pressure, Dr. Venturini was about to say "no, thank you" when he asked Tisha. She ran up to him, cleats in hand. Soon, she was on the field trying out. For the next two years she played on that team.

At thirteen Tisha received her first invitation to the state Olympic Development Program. From there, she made the regional ODP team. At age sixteen the Junior National Team added her name to a roster that included Julie Foudy, Mia Hamm, and Kristine Lilly. The year was 1986. In 1987 Foudy, Hamm, and Lilly joined the Women's National Team. Tisha joined the U-19 National Team— considered the WNT's B team. Often they played each other in tournaments. One in particular stands out. In one game the WNT only beat the U-19 2–0.

Tisha laughs and says, "They were so mad." Next game, WNT players stepped out on the field ready to teach the B team a lesson. They beat them 10–0. "I was marking Joy. She had me running everywhere. I was so exhausted, the coach took me out!"

The first time Tisha Venturini was invited to train with the WNT, she turned them down. The invitation came after a grueling two-week regional ODP camp. She was tired and homesick. Later Tisha realized what made her really turn them down. "I was just plain scared. I didn't think I matched up."

Fortunately Tisha received a second invitation. WNT's coaching staff brought her in to help train the team for the 1991 Women's World Cup. After the win she got lucky. Says Tisha, "Shannon Higgins retired. She happened to be a center midfielder. I slipped right in there. Everything has happened just perfect for me."

ON THE FIELD

Some teammates call her Vench. Others stick to Tish. As an attacking center midfielder, her

main job is receiving and passing the ball so
the forwards can score. "Of course I play
defense, everyone does, but I love to go forward with the ball. That's my strength."

Her California roots have inspired some
teammates to call her laid back. Says Tisha,
"I'll be on the field and someone will make a
move I've never seen before, and I'll go, 'Wow!
how did she do that?'" When that happens,
she's apt to lose concentration and may appear
a little spacy. But sometimes she can't help it.
"I'll get these moments when I look at them
playing on the field and go, 'I can't believe I'm
on this team!'"

Best game moment: If Tisha Venturini could
relive any one moment on the field, it would be
when Shannon MacMillan shot the winning
goal in the 1996 Olympic semifinal game
against Norway. No other moment comes
close. The previous year Norway had snatched
the 1995 Women's World Cup right out of their
hands. Says Tisha, "We knew we were better.
The Olympics was our time to prove it."

Tisha had no doubt they'd win. Even when
Norway took the lead early, she remained
calm. "I can't really explain it, I can only say
that throughout that game, I just kept saying,

'No way are they ruining this for us. We're on home soil in front of 60,000 fans screaming USA!' We were gonna do it. It was just a matter of when."

With minutes remaining in sudden death, Shannon MacMillan's "golden goal" defined "when."

Red card: None.

Superstitions/lucky clothing/rituals: She and Kristine Lilly engage in a private little handshake before each game.

Injuries: During a college game, Tisha broke a bone in her foot that required surgery. A screw was inserted. She resumed playing twenty-two days later and finished her college season at UNC Months later at a WNT camp she reinjured the foot and had to have a second surgery. "This time I took time coming back," says Tisha as she knocks wood. "So far it's just fine."

Jersey number: Tisha wore number 13 through college, but when she joined the WNT, 13 was taken by Kristine Lilly. When Wendy Gebauer retired, Tisha took the number 15.

Blooper: No one blooper stands out. Says Tisha, "I embarrass myself often."

SOCCER IS MY LIFE

At a regional ODP camp a coach stopped then-fourteen-year-old Tisha Venturini as she was boarding the bus to go home and said, "You're gonna make it big time." Was that when she knew soccer had become a major part of her life? Actually, no. That moment happened years earlier when the boys traveling team invited her to join. Tisha knew that in order to improve, she had to play with better players. The boys team offered the only opportunity. "I was so petrified when I walked out there. Those guys did not want to accept me, but once I started playing, everything changed. I wasn't nervous anymore. My love for the game chopped down all the barriers. They knew I loved being on the field, and nothing a teamful of twelve-year-old rowdy boys could say was gonna stop me. We stayed together for two years, and those guys became my best friends."

Though she excelled at several other sports, soccer was always number one. Says Tisha, "I'd get burnt out on volleyball and softball,

but never on soccer. I always loved playing it."
Even during high school, and not because her
team was exceptional. She loved playing with
them because they had so much fun. The low-
pressure environment offered a nice contrast
to her intense ODP experience.

Tisha's mom knew, given the choice, her
daughter would rather practice ball skills
than do anything else, including schoolwork,
which was why house rules remained clear:
grades first, soccer second. "I won't say playing sports helped me be a better student, but
it did help me manage my time, because I
knew if my schoolwork slipped, there was no
soccer."

Shy by nature, Tisha was especially quiet on
her first trip with the Junior National Team.
She had good reason with teammates that
included Julie Foudy, Mia Hamm, Kristine
Lilly, Carla Overbeck, and Joy Biefeld
(Fawcett). Says Tisha, "I used to call them 'the
big studs.' I was scared to death."

On their first trip over to Bulgaria Tisha
kept to herself until Julie Foudy paid her a
visit. "She sat down next to me on the plane
and started talking the way Julie does." The
conversation helped. Tisha began to feel more
comfortable.

Being around other players who juggled academics and soccer was also helpful. On that trip to Bulgaria Tisha noticed how Julie Foudy's nose was always crammed in a book. Says Tisha, "I was getting ready to apply to colleges. Julie's study habits reminded me that not only did I need to be a good player, I needed a decent GPA and SAT scores to get into the good schools."

Tisha attended the University of North Carolina at Chapel Hill, where her game only got better playing next to Mia Hamm for three years and Kristine Lilly for two. In her four years there, the Tar Heels won four NCAA titles. Senior year Tisha Venturini was awarded the Hermann Trophy. Her jersey, number 13, is retired and hangs in UNC's gymnasium next to the retired jerseys of Mia Hamm, Kristine Lilly, April Heinrichs, and Shannon Higgins.

ON INSPIRATION

Tisha Venturini feels blessed to have such a supportive family. When she turned down the WNT's first invitation to attend camp, her parents never said a word. "I think a lot of parents would have said, 'Are you crazy? You can't turn down the national team!' but Mom and Dad knew I'd be miserable. I wasn't ready and they respected that."

No doubt, it was hard for them to zip lips. The Venturinis became soccer fans the moment their children laced on cleats. Her dad's busy medical practice never kept him from the field. Even now, wherever the WNT plays, the Venturinis are usually there watching from the stands. Having a physician close by comes in handy. A few years ago Shannon MacMillan came down with mononucleosis. Dr. Venturini was the one who diagnosed her symptoms.

Tisha wonders how children raised without family support succeed. Says Tisha, "They must really want it badly. To be honest, I'm not sure I could have. I might have given up and said it's not worth it."

ADVICE TO YOUNG ATHLETES

Tisha Venturini doesn't want young players to think losing means you're a loser. "I hate to lose, but it's part of playing sports."

Her advice on the subject is told through a story. After their loss to Norway in the 1995 Women's World Cup, players were mad at themselves and each other. They wanted to retreat, hide away, but they couldn't. A final game for the cup ranking had to be played. They also had a WNT family party scheduled for the following day.

At the party the mood was less then festive until Captain Carla Overbeck took charge. She stood in front of the WNT family brigade and reminded her teammates of a few facts. Surrounding them were family members who did not love them any less for losing. The game was over. It was time to move on. Everyone had tears in their eyes when Carla finished speaking.

Recalling the moment still makes Tisha tear up. She wipes her eyes and says, "Carla put it in perspective. We lost the game, but we still had each other. We were still the Women's National Team. Of course, the next day we went out and kicked butt!"

Tisha also offers advice about sportsmanship. For the past few years she's worked at several soccer camps. Though she loves coaching young players, hearing them yell at each other doesn't thrill her. Says Tisha, "No one means to screw up. If you don't have something positive to say, zip it." Talking trash to opponents is another tactic she hears too often. "Respecting other players is number one. Sure you want to beat the pants off them, but talking trash is unsportsmanlike. Any coach who condones it should be called on the carpet by parents. Beat your opponents fair and square. Don't resort to nastiness on the field. There's no place for it."

★ ★ ★

FACTS

Caps: 111

Goals: 38

Assists: 17

Sponsors: Nike.

Causes: National Spokeswoman, Produce For Better Health Foundation.

Coaching/camps: Julie Foudy Soccer Camp coach; Kristine Lilly Soccer Academy coach.

Awards (partial list): 1991, 1994 NCAA MVP; 1994 Player of the Year; 1994 MAC Award; 1994 Hermann Award; 1996 Olympic Gold Medal; 1998 Goodwill Games Gold Medal.

FAVORITES

Foods: Corn on the cob, candy, cinnamon toast.

Hobbies: Snow- and water-skiing, bike riding, keeping a journal.

Movies: *Father of the Bride, Grease, The American President.*

Movie stars: Tom Cruise, Tom Hanks, Annette Bening, John Travolta.

TV shows: *Just Shoot Me, Home Improvement, Cheers, The Rosie O'Donnell Show.*

Epilogue

After spending a week with these extraordinary young women, it's now easy to understand why, whenever one of them is questioned about her performance, the focus is always shifted back to the team. The anthem of the U.S. Women's National Team could be "the whole is greater than any one part." Every member seems to understand this fact about the team in which many of them have grown up.

Where does the U.S. Women's National Team go from here? "We keep on winning," says Coach Tony DiCicco. "Our goal is to keep on winning forever." Maintaining that goal causes some concern among players, who spoke frankly about it in *All-American Girls*. Mia Hamm expressed it best when she said, "If we want to stay on top, we have to put a league together so players can play full-time.

Otherwise, we're going to lose our lead. It's that simple, really."

On the eve of the 1999 Women's World Cup, hosted one year before the 2000 Olympic Games, the USSF (United States Soccer Federation), this country's soccer governing body, has not yet committed to the formation of a professional women's league even though the men formed a league of their own in 1993.

This soccer mom hopes USSF makes that commitment soon. The ever-growing popularity of the WNBA (Women's National Basketball Association) proves if you give the American public women's teams to cheer for, we will buy tickets. American girls are playing soccer by the millions. They aren't going to stop. Germany, Japan, Norway, and Sweden already have women's semiprofessional and professional leagues in place.

The U.S. Women's National Team is to international women's soccer what Brazil and France are to men's—simply the best. To echo the words spoken often by WNT players in *All-American Girls*, they deserve a league of their own, too.

★ ★ ★

Appendix I

Post–1996 Olympic Team
WNT Players

★ ★ ★

TRACY NOONAN DUCAR

PERSONAL STATS

Position: Goalkeeper
Height: 5'7"
Weight: 135
Birthday: 6/18/73
Sponsor: Adidas
Caps: 20

BRIEF WNT HISTORY

At age twelve, Tracy Noonan reached a cross-roads: should she concentrate on being a forward or a goalkeeper? Until then, she had played both positions. A goalkeeping camp run by her future WNT coach, Tony CiCicco, helped her decide.

Raised in North Andover, Massachusetts, Tracy played on the UNC Tar Heels with Mia Hamm, Kristine Lilly, Tisha Venturini, Cindy Parlow, and Debbie Keller. Mia gave her the name Noodles. Other players call her Noon. Michelle Akers switched to Duke after Tracy's marriage in 1995.

Her road to the Women's National Team began in the Olympic Development Program. At thirteen, she made the ODP Under-14 state team, and though she was always invited to ODP regional camps, Tracy never made the teams.

A serious back injury playing high school basketball sidelined her for one year. Invited to join the WNT's 1996 Olympic training camp, a second back injury kept her from making the final cut. In 1997 she joined the team. Someday she hopes to have children. Tracy smiles. "My husband told me he wants girls because I'd be such a good role model."

Best game moment: Until the early 1990s, the University of North Carolina at Chapel Hill was the undisputed top-ranked women's college soccer team. That changed when other soccer programs caught up. The impact was significant on the goalkeeper's position. Tracy explains, "It used to be keepers didn't do much, then all of a sudden, we weren't winning by five points anymore. We were only winning by one." A career highlight was the 1994 NCAA National Championship played in Portland, Oregon: UNC vs. Notre Dame. At halftime of the final game the Tar Heels were up by one. Says Tracy, "In the second half Notre Dame threw tons of crosses and shots at me. I don't remember the crowd, or the noise, but I remember everything about that game. No matter what they threw at me, I knew I was gonna get it. That was a great game." In both the semifinal and final games, Tracy Noonan (Ducar) recorded shutouts.

Blooper: In one college game played on a football field of long soft grass, a ball came at Tracy which she trapped with one foot, then tripped over with the other. Says Tracy, "The fans were vicious. They screamed, 'How many martinis have you had?' What's worse, the following year, we returned and I did the exact same thing again!"

★　　★　　★

FACTS

Causes/camps: Smoke-Free Kids, a soccer anti-smoking campaign.

Awards: 1994 Olympic Festival All-Star; 1995 UNC captain & MVP; 1995 MAC Award and Hermann Trophy finalist.

FAVORITES

Foods: Skittles, pizza, shrimp, and grits.

Movies: *Dances With Wolves.*

Movie stars: Anthony Hopkins, Robert Redford, Jodie Foster, Harrison Ford.

TV shows: *Just Shoot Me, ER.*

$\star$ $\star$ $\star$

CHRISTIE PEARCE

PERSONAL STATS

Position: Defender
Height: 5'5½"
Weight: 135
Birthday: 6/24/75
Jersey number: 3
Sponsor: Kappa/Lanzera
Caps: 37
Goals: 2
Assists: 2

BRIEF WNT HISTORY

In high school Christie Pearce was hailed as the finest athlete ever produced in Ocean County, New Jersey, and the only one who ever made first team All-County in field hockey, basketball, and soccer. She attended Monmouth University in New Jersey on a basketball scholarship, where she also played varsity soccer.

Her route to the WNT was indirect. Christie explains, "I didn't do ODP, I didn't play club soccer, and I never went to soccer camps when I was little." What she did do was always give one hundred percent when playing sports, an effort WNT coach Tony DiCicco noticed when he watched her play a game coached by his friend—Christie Pearce's soccer coach. The moral of the story? She smiles, "I always tell kids, 'Everytime you go out on the field, be prepared to deliver your best, because you never know who's watching.'"

Soon after he saw her, Tony DiCicco faxed her an invitation to join a WNT training camp. At first she thought it was a mistake. Says Christie, "I wasn't part of the soccer community, so I figured if he invited me, he must have invited lots of players." He didn't. When Christie arrived and discovered one of her suitemates was Mia Hamm, she began to believe maybe Coach DiCicco did see something special. After that camp he called again, this time inviting her to join the WNT for a tournament in Australia. When she told her dad, he cried. "Dad's a great athlete who didn't realize his dreams. The fact that I'm realizing mine has meant so much to him." Christie Pearce played her first international game for WNT on February 28, 1997, in Melbourne, Australia.

Best game moment: For Christie, best game moments happen before each game when the National Anthem plays.

Blooper: Can't recall any.

★　　★　　★

FACTS

Causes/camps: Several free clinics to inner-city youth players; participated in soccer camp at Wyoming Indian reservation.

Awards: 2-time Regional All-American; 2-time New Jersey College Player of the Year; 1996, 1997 Female Athlete of the Year, Monmouth University; holds numerous records in soccer and basketball.

Appendix I

FAVORITES

Foods: Pizza, bagels, buffalo wings.

Movies: *Goodwill Hunting, Grease, My Best Friend's Wedding.*

Movie stars: John Travolta, Brad Pitt, Julia Roberts.

TV shows: *Days of Our Lives, Ally McBeal, Friends.*

KATE SOBRERO

PERSONAL STATS

Position: Defender

Height: 5'7"

Weight: 135

Birthday: 8/23/76

Jersey number: 20

Sponsor: Adidas

Caps: 13

Goals: 0

Assists: 1

BRIEF WNT HISTORY

Kate Sobrero, one of the WNT's newest players, joined her first camp in January 1998. The youngest of four, she is the only girl, which makes her the little princess in her large Italian family. Growing up, she loved soccer but also loved other sports, especially tennis. Her dad's job caused the family to move often. Soccer became a connection to new communities. She joined teams and made friends.

At fourteen, she joined the Olympic Development Program, made the state team immediately, but didn't make the regional team until her high school senior year. That year, she also made the U-20 National Team. Says Kate, "If my story offers inspiration to anyone, it would be to those players who aren't the stars. I always worked hard but was never a highly sought after player."

She attended Notre Dame, but when the coaching staff first approached her, they made it clear she might not start on the team. Kate Sobrero not only started all four years, she earned many accolades, including being hailed as the player whose performance was instrumental in the Fighting Irish's 1995 NCAA Championship win.

A 1997 Dean's List graduate with a degree in science/business, Kate plans to join the corporate world. In fact, she was interviewing for jobs when she got the call to join a WNT camp in the winter of 1998. Her reaction? Says Kate,

"It was so weird to be playing with people whose names and faces are on T-shirts I wear!"

Best game moment: To date, Kate Sobrero's best game moment happened in college, in the final game of the 1995 NCAA championship. She was named player of the game and the tournament. Says Kate, "That game, I definitely played in the zone. I was everywhere!"

Blooper: In the first game of her high school senior year, Kate dribbled the ball down the field with no one near her, tripped, and landed flat on her face. The crowd laughed, she laughed, and her teammates laughed so hard they had trouble reacting to the counterattack. Says Kate, "I am a major klutz and everyone knows it!"

FACTS

Awards: 1994, 1995, 1996 NSCAA All-American; 1995 NCAA Final Four Defensive MVP; 1996 Big East Defensive Player of the Year.

FAVORITES

Foods: Anything with cheese, especially macaroni and cheese.

Hobbies: Reading.

Movies: *Beautiful Girls, Can't Hardly Wait.*

Movie stars: Meg Ryan, Harrison Ford.

TV shows: *90210, Real World, Party of Five,* MTV.

★ ★ ★

The quality of women's soccer in America is reflected by the depth of the National Team Pool. Here are some players to watch in the future.

SUSAN BUSH

Position: Forward
Birthday: 11/10/80
Hometown: Houston, Texas
College: Currently attending St. John's High School. Committed to North Carolina.
First cap: 12/16/98 vs. Ukraine
First goal: None, as of this writing

DANIELLE FOTOPOULOS

Position: Forward
Birthday: 3/24/76
Hometown: Altamonte Springs, Florida

College: University of Florida
First cap: 1/14/96 vs. Russia
First goal: 1/18/96 vs. Ukraine (scored three goals)

SARA WHALEN

Position: Defender/Midfielder
Birthday: 4/28/76
Hometown: Greenlawn, New York
College: University of Connecticut
First cap: 4/24/97 vs. France
First goal: 5/8/98 vs. Iceland

ALY WAGNER

Position: Midfielder
Birthday: 8/10/80
Hometown: San Jose, California
College: Santa Clara
First cap: 12/16/98 vs. Ukraine
First goal: None, as of this writing

★ ★ ★

Appendix II

And Furthermore . . . Soccer Tidbits from WNT Player Interviews

THOUGHTS ON COMPETITION

Carla Overbeck says: "I think it is healthy for young kids. It keeps them involved in something positive and helps them focus."

Joy Fawcett says: "Competition helps develop a strong sense of self."

Shannon MacMillan says: "Competition builds amazing confidence and self-worth!"

Tracy Ducar says: "Competition raises the level of your game. Those who can handle it get better; those who can't, crumble."

Lorrie Fair says: "Competition goes hand in hand with cooperation."

Kate Sobrero says: "Against tough competition, winning is the greatest feeling!"

Michelle Akers says: "Competition defines who you are, what you want, and what you're willing to give."

HOW DO PLAYERS FEEL WHEN NEW PLAYERS JOIN WNT?

Carla Overbeck says: "I welcome them because they are brought into our camps for one reason—to help us win!"

Joy Fawcett says: "You always take note of what position they play. New players make you work harder."

Tiffany Roberts says: "I don't get nervous, but I do compare myself to them."

Tisha Venturini says: "New faces keep things interesting and competitive! When someone joins the team, I gain one more sister!"

Kristine Lilly says: "New players make me step up my game."

Mia Hamm says: "I love it when new players come on the team. I get excited to see how they fit in and how they improve our team."

WHEN NOT IN TRAINING, HOW DO PLAYERS STAY FIT?

Kristine Lilly says: "I run six days a week. Sometimes it's long distance, sprints, stairs. I also do a fitness regime."

Michelle Akers says: "I play with other teams, run, do a fitness regime, and cross-train."

Kate Sobrero says: "I run and kick the ball against the wall."

Tisha Venturini says: "I don't really have a season. I always run sprints, weight train, do a fitness regime and ball work."

Tracy Ducar says: "I do a combination of twenty- to thirty-minute runs and sprints, and a fitness regime."

Tiffany Roberts says: "I try to find a partner to push me. I lift weights, do timed runs, and play with the ball on my own."

Shannon MacMillan says: "I run and train with the University of Portland team."

Joy Fawcett says: "I usually do fitness and hard running three days a week, jog three days a week, lift weights three days a week, and play as much as possible."

Carla Overbeck says: "I run, lift, sprint, work on agility and ball skills."

IMPROVING-YOUR-GAME TIPS

Tiffany Roberts says: "Set goals for yourself early."

Tracy Ducar says: "Set short- and long-term goals. I call them performance and outcome goals. For example, if a long-term goal is to join a club team, a short-term goal might be increase your juggling. If you juggled twenty-five one day, then the next time you juggle, shoot for twenty-six or above. Also, make sure to post performance and outcome goals where you can see them. Be realistic, but push yourself!"

Kate Sobrero says: "Practice makes perfect!"

Julie Foudy says: "Success happens to those who love what they do."

Michelle Akers says: "Try harder every day."

Joy Fawcett says: "You can do anything you want to do. It just takes a lot of hard work and determination!"

DIET DURING THE SEASON

Says Carla Overbeck: "I eat healthy most of the time, but I love chocolate. I can't help it!"

Says Joy Fawcett: "I try to be more aware of

eating healthy, but I still eat junk food. I also try to drink more water."

Says Tiffany Roberts: "I don't really have one except I like to eat a lot of carbs like pasta, rice, and potatoes."

Says Kristine Lilly: "Lots of water!"

Says Mia Hamm: "I try to have a healthy balanced diet that contains carbs, fruits and veggies, protein, and plenty of water!"

Says Tisha Venturini: "I eat healthy all the time. You really can't get lazy and eat whatever during the off season. It doesn't work that way."

A PERSONALITY TRAIT TROUBLESOME ON THE FIELD

Says Lorrie Fair: "Sometimes I try to do too much, like I'll dribble too much or try to make a difficult pass instead of a simple one."

Says Julie Foudy: "If the game isn't competitive, I get bored and start to goof off with Carla."

Says Mia Hamm: "My intensity."

Says Michelle Akers: "Too aggressive. Too competitive."

Says Shannon MacMillan: "Looking for the meg!"

★ ★ ★

About the Author

MARLA MILLER is a writer, columnist, and radio talk show host during the week, but on the weekends, she's a carpooling soccer mom. She lives in Newport Beach, California, with her husband, Terry Mazura, and their three daughters. Visit her at http://www.allamericangirlsoccer.com.

WNBA

STARS OF WOMEN'S BASKETBALL

Take to the courts with league MVP Cynthia Cooper. Go eye to eye with unblinking Sheryl Swoopes. Pound the boards with superstar and supermodel Lisa Leslie. And see what's *really* happening in the red-hot game of women's basketball! Here's everything you need to know about the teams—and the players—that are putting the bad-boy superstars of the NBA in their place. Packed with photos, stats, profiles, interviews, team spotlights, and Q&As, this slam-dunking book tells the amazing stories behind these phenomenal players.

INSIDE STORIES YOU WON'T SEE ANYWHERE ELSE!

by James Ponti

Now available!

An Archway Paperback
Published by Pocket Books